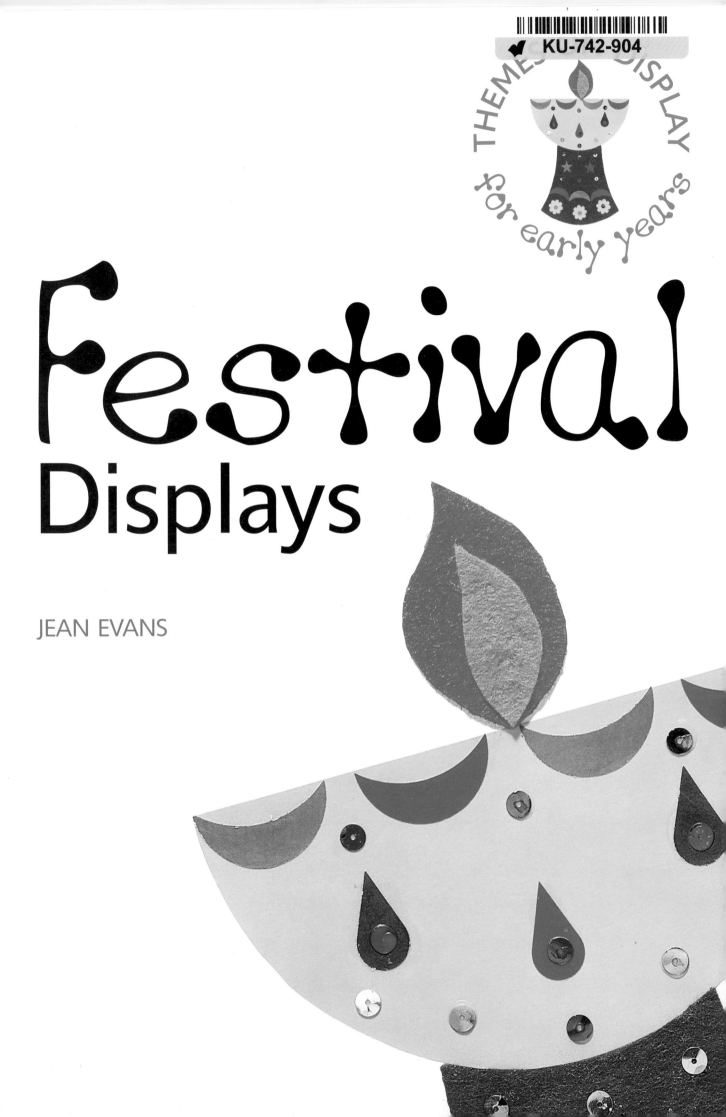

THEMES FOR DISPLAY for early years

Festival
Displays

JEAN EVANS

AUTHOR JEAN EVANS

EDITOR SUSAN HOWARD

ASSISTANT EDITOR SAVERIA MEZZANA

SERIES DESIGNER LYNNE JOESBURY

DESIGNER SARAH ROCK

ILLUSTRATIONS CATHY HUGHES

PHOTOGRAPHS PENNY SHEPHERD

With thanks to the staff and children of the following nurseries who helped with the displays: Whinney Banks Nursery, Middlesborough; Castle View Nursery, Chester-le-Street; Little Learners Nursery, Scorton; Kids & Co Nursery, Darlington; Bow Preparatory School, Durham.
Special thanks to Sue Welburn and her staff for their additional input to many of the displays.

Designed using Adobe Pagemaker

Published by Scholastic Ltd, Villiers House, Clarendon Avenue, Leamington Spa, Warwickshire CV32 5PR

Visit our website at www.scholastic.co.uk

Text © Jean Evans
© 2001 Scholastic Ltd

1 2 3 4 5 6 7 8 9 0   1 2 3 4 5 6 7 8 9 0

British Library Cataloguing-in-Publication Data
A catalogue record for this book is available from the British Library.

ISBN 0-439-01812-9

Contents

Introduction

The importance of display

The creation of displays is an integral part of any early years setting. Displays provide staff with an ideal way of demonstrating how much they value children's work and their individual contributions to the group. They also present further learning opportunities related to a specific theme which can effectively link all areas of the curriculum.

Every display in this book offers several stimulating and interesting ways of involving the children. *Festivals* is divided into four chapters, each focusing on a different season.

Chapter one explores spring festivals, beginning logically with a stimulus display about new life related to Easter. The theme of new life is continued as children grow seeds and small trees for the festivals, Ching Ming on page 20 and Naw-Ruz on page 28.

The natural elements of fire and water are represented creatively for displays on Holi (page 18) and Pesach (page 24). Children are encouraged to talk about the importance of giving to others as they work on displays for Mother's Day (page 26) and Eid-ul-Fitr (page 16).

Chapter two has an exciting selection of colourful displays related to summer festivals. Following on from the stimulus display about May Day on page 31, children can enjoy creating a large elephant for the festival of Wesak (page 32), colourful boats for the Dragon Boat Festival (page 34) and attractive kites for Japanese Children's Day (page 44).

Chapter three is related to autumn festivals and many of these focus on harvest. Children are encouraged to compare fruit and vegetables from around the world and create their own harvest baskets.

Many of the displays in this chapter involve three-dimensional work. For example, for the Jewish festival, Sukkot (page 52), children will enjoy creating their own hut beneath the wall display. They will be able to have a go at making drums to celebrate the Ethiopian New Year (page 46), clay diva lamps for Divali (page 54), and megaphones for Rosh Hashanah (page 50).

THEMES ON DISPLAY
for early years

Chapter four concludes the yearly cycle with winter festivals. A candle display sets the scene leading to the Jewish festival of light, Hanukkah (page 60). A home-made Advent calendar (page 62) provides excitement as the children anticipate Christmas, and their paintings of the traditional story are creatively transformed into an original interactive display. A bird's Christmas tree containing home-made bird feeders reinforces the message of caring for living things in winter (page 72).

Religious festivals and cultural events

The beliefs and values of different nations throughout the world are expressed through their religious festivals, celebrations and traditional customs. Exploring these events often extends into a study of different cultural lifestyles. As children take part in the activities associated with the displays in this book, they will begin to make comparisons with their own lifestyles and develop a respect for their own culture and beliefs as well as those of others.

The festivals and celebrations chosen for the displays in this book represent many of the world's religions as well as some secular events. It is important to remember, however, that some religions use lunar calendars or other methods of calculation to decide the exact date when a particular festival will occur, and so some dates vary from year to year. It is advisable, therefore, to check the precise date using a reliable source such as *The Shap Calendar of Religious Festivals* available from The Shap Working Party on World Religions, c/o The National Society's RE Centre, 36 Causton Street, London SW1P 4AU, tel: 020-79321194.

Aims of this book

This book will enable adults working in a variety of pre-school settings to plan, set up and use a range of visually stimulating displays related to different festivals. The book will form an invaluable resource during long-term planning to ensure that a range of festivals and events are included and effectively represented.

The most important participants in the creation of the displays are the children. Remember to involve them as much as possible at every stage of the project, and always let them help to choose colours and materials. As far as safety allows, let them explore the displays freely and only interact to make suggestions, answer questions and develop their ideas further by extending resources.

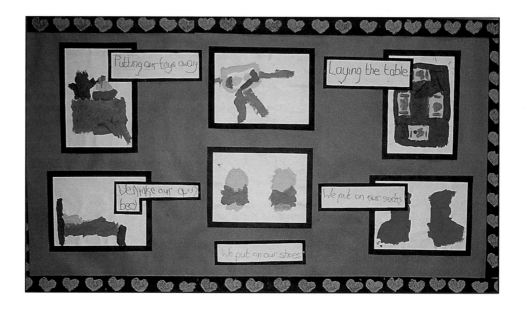

The displays
There are three types of
display in this book.
● Stimulus displays
The aim of this type of
display is to stimulate the
interest of children and
parents at the start of
each season of festivals. It
could be something that
the adults in the nursery
set up as an introduction
to the season, such as the
'Candles' display on page
59, which provides a
general introduction to
the winter festivals
displays in Chapter 4. It
might involve children
and carers by asking
them to bring in
contributions to add to
one of your displays, such
as the 'Easter and new
life' display on page 15,
which suggests that
children bring in toy
rabbits and lambs.

Each stimulus display
page includes a list of
resources, instructions for
making the display, ideas for talking
points and suggestions for home links.
● Interactive displays
Children learn by experience and
exploration, so the aim of these displays
is to provide them with the opportunity
to do this. They will be able to handle
artefacts from other cultures and to
make comparisons with familiar objects
from their own environment.

Many of the interactive displays
provide sensory experiences and
encourage the children to express their
feelings and use their imagination. From
these interactive experiences, using
resources arranged on tables, the
children will develop their own ideas.
The accompanying wall display will
stimulate their natural curiosity and
extend their knowledge further.

Each interactive display begins with
brief details of the background and
customs associated with the festival and
has the following sub-headings:
Learning objectives – These
highlight the main purpose of the
display in the context of the Early

Learning Goals. The common aim
running through all displays is to raise
children's awareness of their own
cultures and beliefs and those of others.
What you need – This section
provides a list of resources needed to
complete the display. These are
generally easily obtained and often
involve parents and children in their
collection. As with the displays
themselves, they are flexible and should
be adapted to suit the needs of
individual groups.
What to do – This section gives a
step-by-step guide to setting up the
displays. Colour schemes are suggested
and advice on appropriate materials to
use is given. Again, these are only
suggestions and should be used as a
basis for discussion into appropriate
choices for your own setting.
Talk about – This section provides
suggestions for discussion, and questions
to ask both during the production of the
display and afterwards, to encourage
the children to express their own ideas
and opinions.

THEMES ON DISPLAY for early years

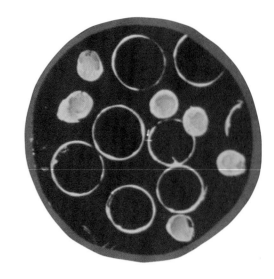

Home links – Parents and carers have an important part to play in their child's development and, with this in mind, every display has suggestions for home links. These might include inviting carers, parents or other family members to talk to the children about something related to the focus of the display. For example, the World Environment Day display on page 42 suggests inviting parents to bring in rubbish for recycling. Other suggestions include encouraging parents to take their children to visit a bottle bank and inviting a parent to talk about gardening.

Using the display – Suggestions on ways to effectively use each display to promote different learning goals within the six areas of learning are included in this section. These suggestions provide excellent activity ideas when planning a mini topic around the festival. The learning areas are Personal, social and emotional development; Communication, language and literacy; Mathematical development; Knowledge and understanding of the world; Physical development and Creative development.

Photocopiable sheets are included at the back of the book. These support and extend the displays in the book, and can be sent home with the children so that they can try out some activities with their families. It is essential that parents and carers are encouraged to be involved with the whole process of creating the displays and to spend some time with their children exploring them.

● Table-top displays

Table-top displays provide opportunities for further exploration on a particular aspect of a festival, without the accompanying wall display. As well as advice on setting up the table, each page includes further table display ideas based on the same festival so that learning opportunities can be extended.

For example, the 'Easter bonnets' table-top display on page 30, which supplements the 'Easter and new life' stimulus display on page 15, provides children with the opportunity to explore different materials as they create their own Easter bonnets.

Further suggestions are made to enable the bonnets to be mounted as an attractive additional wall display or to convert the table into a card- or nest-making activity.

Planning displays

When planning a festival display, it is important to work as a whole staff. Begin by making a list of available spaces for the display, their location, size and position, and choose the most appropriate. Refer to long-term plans to decide on the proposed festival and plan a brainstorming session for suggested extension activities to relate to each of the six areas of learning.

Make a decision about where the final display will be sited and ensure that all the necessary resources are in supply. Make a rough sketch of the proposed display, considering points made in each of the following paragraphs. An easy way to do this is to make a list of the paragraph headings and work through them systematically, asking appropriate questions as you do so.

Setting up the displays

It is essential, when taking down old displays, that the display board or surface is thoroughly cleared of pins, scraps of paper and staples so that there is a smooth surface to begin the next display. All too often, displays are mounted on boards which have half-pulled-out staples and left-over pins in them. This can cause injury to fingers.

Background papers

Plain frieze paper is usually the best form of backing paper, but wallpaper can be used to create a particular effect, for example when creating the display

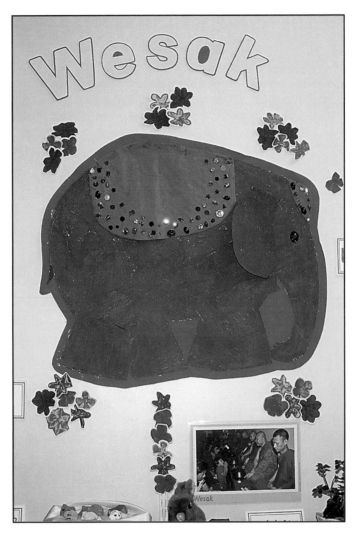

about Pancake Day on page 70 to represent the walls of a room, or when a certain texture would be appropriate, such as a blown vinyl sea for the dragon boats (page 34) to sail across. Newspaper can create a very effective background, for example as part of the Shavuot display on page 36, to represent scrolls, or when using recycled materials for the World Environment Day display on page 42.

Colours

Consider the overall effect of colours used in a display at the planning stage. If the display is full of large collage work and labels, such as the Raksha Bandhan display on page 38, it is usually best to choose a plain colour for the background so that the actual work displayed stands out. When the background forms part of a scene, such as sky and grass, blue and green will be the main colours but these can be enhanced by sponge-painting different

shades of the same colour to build up layers on the paper.

Certain colours are associated with different temperatures. Use appropriate colours, such as red and orange to represent the flames in the Holi display on page 18, and blue and purple for the dark sky in the Eid-ul-Fitr display on page 16.

Mounting

It is important for children to see that their work is valued, and this can be achieved through careful mounting of pictures before they are attached to the display board. Ensure that the work is neatly trimmed to remove rough edges and mount this on paper, leaving a border showing. The size of this border will vary according to the size of the picture. Mounts can be in direct contrast with the background paper, or black so that they stand out.

Children's work looks particularly effective when mounted on paper which matches the title lettering and contrasts with the background. For really special pictures, try double-mounting so that there are two borders with the one nearest the picture matching the display background.

Finished mounted work can be attached directly to the display with a staple gun, or stuck to a small box before being glued to the display board to create a 3-D effect.

Labels, captions and titles

All labelling should be clear and consistent. Young children are just becoming familiar with print as a form of communication, so it is best to stick to simple lower case lettering with upper case only at the start of sentences and for the initial letters of names.

If possible, use a computer to print out lettering to achieve consistency. Make letters large enough to see at a reasonable distance. Alternatively, use stencils or draw around large wooden or plastic letters. Drawing letters free-hand is difficult and, if this is done, it is better to rule lines as guides to ensure that the letters are the same height. Make sure that the spaces between each word are the same.

Black lettering stands out, particularly for the title of the display, but sometimes coloured lettering which matches the mounts on the pictures is effective. When choosing colours for lettering and mounts, ensure that the chosen colour is a direct contrast to the background paper so that it is easy to see. Once the lettering is printed, it can be cut out and mounted on white or coloured paper, or glued directly onto the background.

Borders

An attractive border finishes off a display effectively. Try varying the border on each display. Commercially-produced

borders can be easily obtained from early years catalogues. They are available in a variety of shades and textures and with plain and scalloped edges. In addition, themed borders are useful, for example, 'icicles' for winter festivals. Home-decorating shops often sell odd rolls of border paper cheaply and these sometimes relate to festival symbols, such as flowers and animals. It is a good idea to build up a stock of these as they become available.

Odd rolls of wallpaper can be bought cheaply and sliced into border rolls. Textured papers such as wood chip and blown vinyl are very effective, and appropriate wrapping paper can be cut into strips to create unusual borders.

Children enjoy creating their own borders using techniques such as printing, for example, the fruit prints surrounding the 'Harvest around the world' display on page 45. This can be done easily on low displays, but for higher displays the background paper needs to be cut to the shape of the display board beforehand so that the children can print the border before it is hung up.

Sponge can easily be cut into the desired shapes. Alternatively, try printing with potatoes or small plastic dough cutters. Sponge paint-rollers come in various sizes and designs, and can be rolled along the paper to create an unusual borders. Try layering colours for an interesting effect.

Home-made borders are instantly attractive. Always involve the children in decision-making when making borders, and try to use their suggestions whenever possible.

Fixing

The most effective way of fixing the background paper to the display board is with a staple gun. However, if this method is used, care must be taken to remove all staples carefully after the display is taken down, preferably using a staple extractor. Alternatively, large drawing pins can be used, but these must be pushed well into the board to avoid the danger of children pulling them out. Once the backing paper is in place, it is best to attach paper and card display items with glue, while thicker items, such as fabric, should be secured with PVA glue rather than pins, to prevent the ends from curling. Sticky-tape loops can also be used for fixing small items, such as boxes.

Joseph

Groups without display boards might find it useful to use portable pieces of pinboard. Take care to secure any free-standing boards so that they do not fall over. Try lodging them behind bricks or tables, and stress that the children must not pull at the board.

3-D displays
3-D effects are attractive and add interest to your displays. They can be created on the board by gluing some items to small boxes so that they stand out from the rest of the work, or by padding out parts of the display, putting newspaper behind them. Larger boxes can be attached from behind using drawing pins or staples.

Table-top displays can be more visually stimulating by arranging objects on different levels. This can be achieved by positioning foam or plastic bricks on the table before draping the fabric over. If the fabric is pinned to the base of the display board, it can then be draped across the gap between the wall and the table to create a continuous effect. The 'Harvest baskets' table-top display on page 58 uses different levels by applying this method.

Create added interest by using different levels and shapes. Have tables of different heights, or include floor space. Use circular, square and rectangular tables and put boxes and bricks on them to display items.

Using structural features
Exciting displays can be created in unusual spaces and by making use of structural features, such as window sills, doors, stair rails, pillars and pipes. Use recessed windows to create scenes. The Nativity display (page 64) and the Chinese New Year display (page 66) were created on a large window sill, and the effect of the light shining from behind resulted in interesting changes of colour and shade.

Create added interest by mounting pictures on the backs of doors and make use of stair rails to hang mobiles.

Covering awkward areas
Drapes are very effective to cover the more unsightly aspects of some rooms, such as pipes, flaking wallpaper and damp patches. Position a table in front of the drape so that it can be put over it in folds to become incorporated into the display. Awkward corners can be treated in a similar way.

Semi-permanent and moveable displays
Some groups have no permanent display space and all equipment has to be stored away after use. If this is the case, make use of trolleys to arrange items on and hang a portable cardboard display of children's work along the front. Look around for any mobile vertical surfaces, such as the

backs of book display racks and home corner screens.

Displays in different rooms

Consider the importance of displays in all rooms, not just the main activity room used by the children. Create simple displays about personal hygiene in the children's toilets. Cover these with sticky-backed plastic to protect them. Position displays about food, healthy eating, table manners and safe handling of food near to where children have meals or snacks.

Do not have displays in kitchens, other than laminated posters, for health and safety reasons. Remember that displays in staff and parents' rooms are equally important – ensure that they are instantly attractive and of high quality.

Outdoor displays

Think about using your outdoor environment to extend your display area. Fences and walls are ideal surfaces on which to create murals related to outdoor topics, such as wildlife or the changing seasons. If possible, involve local art colleges in the production of your outdoor displays.

Photographs

Remember the importance of photographs as a means of explaining to parents the learning objectives that you propose to cover through planned activities and displays, to help children to recall a sequence of events, and as a means of evaluating work and making modifications for future plans.

Take photographs of the preparation of each display: the children painting, making collage pictures, the staff preparing the background and so on. If the work involves an additional feature, such as a walk around the setting or local area to look at bins, as

one of the activities related to World Environment Day on page 42, take photographs of this. The collection of photographs can then be used as an additional display or to make a book. Add appropriate explanations about each stage which will be of interest to either staff, parents or children, according to the purpose of the book.

Artefacts

As with all topic work, for every festival, it is useful to begin to collect together a box of artefacts for future displays. Add to these by making requests to parents and people from the locality. Hang up a list of suggested items required or send home a letter. Unusual artefacts can sometimes be borrowed. Some towns

have multicultural centres which have loan schemes. Holidays are good times to buy or find resources relating to different customs and cultures. Markets are an ideal place to pick up pieces of fabric and sometimes traditional clothes.

Sources of free information and resources

Make appropriate use of local recycling centres and businesses for free or cheap materials. You will find that many local firms are only too willing to support early years settings, and will gladly donate items which can be used in your display work.

Printers often supply paper offcuts free of charge if you are willing to collect them, and they can also be a useful source for different types of paper and cardboard. Ask carers to donate old clothing or furniture catalogues, holiday brochures and empty clean containers. Also, search through your out-of-date catalogues from early years suppliers for appropriate pictures that the children can cut out and stick into home-made books.

Books

Make appropriate use of libraries to extend your book supply. Often librarians will suggest suitable fiction or non-fiction titles relating to a given culture or festival. Try to involve the children in making their own books as often as possible and hang these next to the display using cup hooks and loops of string. Use a favourite religious story as a display stimulus.

It is useful to build up your own library of reference books and story-books relating to multicultural festivals. Some good starting-points are *Children Just Like Me* by Barnabas and Anabel Kindersley (*Celebration!* series Dorling Kindersley) and

the *Festivals Through the Year* series (Heinemann). Brief background information for each display is given in this book, but you will find it useful to have your own sources of reference.

Lighting

Consider how the light falling on a display can alter its appearance, creating beautiful effects. Make use of natural light by placing displays in windows, covering them with coloured Cellophane and/or coloured tissue. Stained-glass windows are particularly effective.

Safety

Always make sure that children handle tools and materials safely, under appropriate supervision. Use staple guns away from children and do not let young children handle staples and drawing pins. Ensure that children only work on the display at floor level and do not have to stand on chairs to reach it. Seek advice from the fire department about materials to use for displays in entrance halls, stairs and corridors.

Spring festivals

Easter and new life

On Easter Sunday, Christians remember the resurrection of Jesus, who died on the cross on Good Friday. Easter is a time to celebrate the rebirth of nature as plants begin to grow again after the winter. The word 'Easter' comes from the name of the Saxon goddess of spring, Eostre. Eggs and chicks are associated with the festival as they signify the appearance of new life. Christian children decorate hard-boiled eggs and exchange chocolate eggs.

Learning objective: to become aware of the changing seasons and the passing of time.

What you need
White backing paper; green tissue paper; cotton wool; painting and drawing equipment; sponges; collage materials including egg-boxes, fur fabric, straw and foil; plant pots; small branches (**NB** Use fallen branches); pipe-cleaners; Plasticine; Easter objects such as feathers, toy chicks and miniature eggs; yellow fabric; spring flowers and twigs.

What to do
Ask the children to sponge-paint a blue sky on white backing paper. When dry, add cotton wool clouds, then mount the paper on the board. Paint on green hills, then cut grass from green tissue paper to stick across the bottom of the board. Using the selection of collage materials, invite children to make spring

animals and plants for your display. These could include chicks, birds in nests, rabbits, blossom trees, daffodils and so on. Nearby, position a table covered with yellow fabric. Let the children help to make 'Easter trees'. Anchor sticks into plant pots using lumps of Plasticine, then encourage the children to hang foil-covered eggs, feathers and small Easter chicks from the branches using pipe-cleaners. Arrange the trees on the table with vases of spring flowers and twigs.

Talk about
● Talk about the signs of spring. Compare them with the signs that tell us that other seasons are approaching.
● Discuss the significance of Easter eggs.

Home links
● Let the children make Easter cards to give to family members.
● Ask parents and carers to encourage their children to bring in a few spring flowers to add to your display.

The vibrancy and colour of spring are captured in the displays in this chapter. Celebrate new beginnings by involving the children in making colourful displays about a variety of spring festivals including Easter, Eid-ul-Fitr and Baisakhi.

Eid-ul-Fitr

Muslims celebrate Eid-ul-Fitr to mark the end of Ramadan, the period of fasting. Eid begins with the new moon during the tenth month of the Muslim calendar. The prophet Mohammed (Peace Be Upon Him) first began to hear messages from the God Allah during the month of Ramadan. To remember this event, Muslims do not eat or drink between sunrise and sunset throughout this month. Usually, they break their fast at sunset by eating a date or apricot with a glass of water. During the fasting, Muslims remember those less fortunate than themselves and often donate to the poor. On the morning of Eid, women stay at home to pray while the men go to the Mosque to say prayers, hear a sermon and greet one another saying, 'Eid Mubarak' ('Holiday Blessings'). After prayers, Muslims visit friends and relatives, exchange Eid gifts, cards and money and enjoy a meal during the day.

Learning objectives: to become aware of the passing of time; to talk about, recognize and recreate simple patterns.

What you need

Black frieze paper; purple and white paper; textured wallpaper; paint in various colours including gold and yellow; star-shaped sponges; glitter; coloured crayons; scissors; felt-tipped pens; cardboard tubes; foil; coloured card; black fabric; *Children Just Like Me* by Barnabas and Anabel Kindersley (*Celebration!* series, Dorling Kindersley); *Eid-ul-Fitr* by Susheila Stone (*Celebration* series, A & C Black); resources associated with Eid (available from Religion in Evidence, tel: 0800-318686).

What to do

Share the books and resources with the children. Discuss the customs associated with Eid, then invite the children to help you make a colourful display which shows some of the items and customs that are associated with the festival.

Back your display board with black paper. Attach to it a large mosque shape cut from purple paper. Cut hexagons from wallpaper and invite the children to draw patterns on them using crayons. Stick them onto the mosque, linking them together to form 'bricks'.

Show the children how to make symmetrical patterns by painting one half of a hexagon shape and then folding the sides together and pressing gently. Once the hexagons are dry, help the children to attach them to the display around the mosque.

Ask the children to paint a large moon shape and some stars using yellow paint. Before the paint dries, sprinkle on glitter to make the stars twinkle. Stick the shapes to the display. Invite the children to make Eid greeting cards by sticking foil moons, stars and other symmetrical patterns onto folded card. Add these to the display.

Make a border using patterned handprints. Ask the children to draw around their hands on white paper, then help them to cut out the shapes. Invite them to use felt-tipped pens to decorate the handprints with symmetrical patterns.

Print patterns onto black fabric using star-shaped sponges and gold paint, and use this to cover a table. Make money boxes by covering kitchen-roll tubes with foil and place these on the table. Add dolls dressed in Muslim costumes and your collection of books, cards and artefacts.

Talk about
● Discuss with the children the phases of the moon and how the new moon signifies the end of Ramadan and the start of Eid celebrations.
● Talk about Eid customs including dressing in best clothes, enjoying family

Using the display
Personal, social and emotional development
● Compare different places of worship. Visit a church, a temple and a mosque.
● Talk about the features of a mosque such as the dome and minaret, or tower where the call to prayer is sounded.
● Discuss other special days. How do the children feel when they are waiting for events such as a birthday or Christmas?

Communication, language and literacy
● Make a book about, or dramatize, daily routines following the sequence from getting up to going to bed.

Mathematical development
● Visit or look at pictures of Muslim mosques. Talk about the patterns on walls and tiles. Find similar patterns on wallpaper and wrapping paper to add to your display.
● Look for tiles around your setting. Talk about how the shapes fit together, or tessellate. Provide shape templates for the children to tessellate.
● Photocopy the 'Phases of the moon' photocopiable sheet on page 73 onto card. Colour the pictures and laminate the sheet, then cut out the individual cards. Invite children to put the moon pictures in sequence.

Creative development
● Make a model mosque from a large cardboard box. Create a dome from an upturned bowl and a minaret from a small box.

feasts and exchanging gifts. Compare with festivals familiar to the children.

Home links
● Ask carers to show their children the moon throughout the month and to help them draw it once a week, comparing the drawings at the end of the month.

THEMES ON DISPLAY
for early years

Holi

Holi falls between late February and April and is the Hindu festival of new beginnings and harvest. Various stories are associated with the festival. One remembers the legend of King Hiranyakashup who ordered all Hindus to worship him as their God. His son Prahlad refused, so the king asked his sister Holika (who could not be harmed by fire) to take Prahlad into a blazing fire. Holika died, but Prahlad survived due to his faith in the real Hindu God. Coconuts are often included in Hindu ceremonies and are thrown on bonfires at Holi to symbolize Prahlad's survival in the fire.

The night before Holi, fires are lit to burn anything bad from the past and to look forward to a brighter future. Holi is also known as 'The Festival of Colour' and Hindus remember how their Lord Krishna used to play in the water with his friend Radha by splashing and squirting her. Today, people remember Krishna by throwing coloured water and paint over one another.

Learning objective: to explore colour in two and three dimensions.

What you need
Backing paper; neutral and coloured sugar paper; scissors; glue; coloured water; paintbrushes; plastic bottles; pumps; spray bottles; coloured powder paint; red and yellow paints; sponge; protective cloth; aprons; yoghurt pots; shallow trays; gold paper.

What to do
Cover a display board with backing paper. Discuss the customs associated with the festival of Holi. Tell the children that they are going to have some fun making their own colourful pictures. Lay a large sheet of neutral sugar paper on the floor and draw around two children to make child-sized outlines. Cut out the shapes and lay them on a protective sheet. Put on aprons and roll up sleeves before letting the children have fun splashing the paper with coloured water using the sprays, brushes and plastic bottles. Before the water dries, invite the children to sprinkle powder paint onto the outlines. Mount the finished figures on contrasting paper before attaching to the display board.

Cover a table with a protective cloth. Provide paper cut into flame shapes, and small quantities of red and yellow powder paint in cut-down yoghurt pots. Invite the children to mix the paint in the shallow trays and then to paint colourful flames. When the shapes are dry, mount them on contrasting paper and display them around the figures.

Complete your display with a heading cut from gold paper.

Talk about
● Discuss the way that the colours merge when powder paint is thrown on the watery outlines.
● Talk about bonfires. Describe their smell, the crackling noises that they make and the heat that they generate. Reinforce the dangers of bonfires.

Home links
● Send home an information sheet telling the story of Lord Krishna and Radha for parents to read to their children.
● If possible, invite an adult from the Hindu community to talk about Holi and the traditions associated with it.

Using the display
Personal, social and emotional development
● At Holi, people clean their homes. Talk about 'spring cleaning'. Clean your setting together, sharing jobs such as washing equipment, sweeping and dusting.
● Talk about the fun that Hindu children have at Holi and how excited they feel. What makes the children excited? Scribe their sentences and add them to the display.

Communication, language and literacy
● Make a list of words associated with bonfires. Use them to make up a group poem.

Knowledge and understanding of the world
● Show the children a coconut and talk about how it feels and looks. Extract and taste its milk. Now break it in half and smell it. (**NB** Check for nut allergies before starting this activity. Coconut is very hard, so do not give pieces to very young children to taste.)

● Observe how colour changes using food colourings and coffee filters. With an eye-dropper, drop the colour onto a filter. Drop another colour next to it and watch the colours merge and change.
● Stand some white carnations in water. Add a few drops of food colouring to the water and observe the flowers each day for a week. What happens to the colour of the petals? You could take pictures each day and compare them at the end of the week.

Physical development
● Enjoy dancing to Indian music, waving streamers and playing drums and tambourines.
● Try moving and dancing like bonfire flames. Make up a short movement sequence to some suitable music such as Stravinsky's 'The Fire Bird'.

Creative development
● Dramatize the story of Lord Krishna and Radha using confetti or small paper scraps to represent paint.
● Explore paint charts. Make your own colour charts by mixing primary colours to create new colours.

Ching Ming

Ching Ming, meaning 'clear and bright', is celebrated by the Chinese as the start of spring and new life. It either falls at the end of their second month, the Budding Moon month, or at the start of the third month, the Sleepy Moon month, which places it in April. The Chinese traditionally visit the tombs of their ancestors at this time and show respect for the dead. Another name for this festival is Chih Shu Chien, which means 'tree-planting festival'. Many Chinese hold a tree-planting ceremony at home or in public. During Ching Ming, people fly kites, which are decorated in bright colours and usually in the shape of creatures such as dragons, birds, snakes and goldfish.

Learning objective: to develop fine and large motor skills using a range of resources and techniques.

What you need
Pale blue frieze paper; contrasting border roll; textured wallpaper; white sugar paper; scissors; glue; sticky tape; garden canes; coloured plastic; white and coloured fabric; string; ribbons; collage materials; colouring materials; coloured tissue paper; table; fabric; selection of plants; plant pots; small seedlings; cress seeds; watering can; small gardening tools; packets of seeds; information books and story-books about plants, such as *Broad Bean* by Christine Back and Barrie Watts (A & C Black) and *The Tiny Seed* by Eric Carle (Puffin Books).

What to do

Cover a display board with pale blue paper and add a border. Ask the children to help you create a colourful display which illustrates the customs associated with the Chinese festival of Ching Ming.

Cut white paper into cloud shapes and invite the children to stick on scraps of white textured wallpaper. Attach the clouds to the display board. Make some colourful kites for your display. For each kite, tape two canes together to make a cross shape and lay the cross onto a piece of coloured plastic, fabric or paper. Cut around the plastic, fabric or paper to create a diamond shape and tape securely to the cross.

Encourage each child to attach a length of string to the end of their kite shape and then help them tie ribbons or twisted coloured tissue at intervals along it. Invite the children to decorate their kites using pens, paints, glitter and collage materials.

Invite the children to have a go at making kites in different shapes, such as goldfish, dragons, snakes and birds. Mount some of the kites on the display and suspend others above it. Add a title and key word labels such as 'fly', 'wind' and 'cloud'.

Place a fabric-covered table in front of your display board. Add a selection of plants, a watering can and packets of seeds. Help the children to plant cress seeds in small pots and put these on the table. Try to include some tree seedlings, such as sycamore.

Display gardening tools and a watering can, and include story-books and information books. Make labels for the different types of plants and seedlings on the table.

Talk about

● Discuss different weather conditions. What conditions are needed to fly a kite? What would happen to the kite if there was no wind?
● Talk about the seeds that the children have planted. What conditions will they need in order to grow?

Home links

● Ask parents and carers to look for signs of new life, such as shoots and buds, when they are out with their children.

Using the display
Personal, social and emotional development

● Talk about the importance of watering plants. Choose a different child each day to take responsibility for watering the seedlings.
● Talk about how Chinese people remember special people who have died in their families. Discuss sensitively how the children feel about their own special relatives.

Communication, language and literacy

● Read stories about growing plants, such as *Sam Plants a Sunflower* by Kate Petty (Macmillan Children's Books), *The Tiny Seed* by Eric Carle (Puffin Books), or *Tilda's Seeds* by Melanie Eclare (Ragged Bears Publishing). Talk about the sequence of growth.

Knowledge and understanding of the world

● Make 2-D kites from canes and fabric, and 3-D kites from tubes and thin fabric, similar to a windsock. Fly them outside on a windy day. Which type of kite is most effective?
● Copy the 'Growth of a seed' photocopiable sheet on page 74 onto card. Colour in the pictures and laminate the sheet, then cut out the individual cards. Invite the children to sequence the pictures to show the growth of a seed.

Physical development

● Find out about tree-planting events in your locality. Let the children help to dig the soil, prepare the plot and plant a tree in your local area, or in the grounds of your setting.
● Pretend to be a conker buried in the soil. Stretch slowly as you grow into a sapling and then into a big tree with branches that wave in the wind.

Creative development

● Make 3-D models of birds, dragons, and goldfish by covering cardboard boxes with brightly-coloured tissue paper, Cellophane and foil.

THEMES ON DISPLAY
for early years

Baisakhi

The three-day festival of Baisakhi is celebrated by Sikhs in April, and is the start of their New Year. Sikhs remember how, in 1699 on Baisakhi Day, the tenth leader Guru Gobind Singh created the 'Khalsa', the strong Sikh brotherhood who would defend the weak and be loyal to their faith. The first two days of the festival are spent reading the Sikh Holy Book, the Guru Granth Sahib, and on the third day, anyone who wants to join the 'Khalsa' must go through an initiation ceremony. First, they must drink amrit, a special sugared water, and then receive the 'five Ks': Kesh (uncut beard and hair); Kangha (a comb to fix the hair in place); Kara (a steel bracelet worn on the right wrist); Kirpan (a short sword); Kachera (a pair of shorts). Together with a turban, these five items make up the uniform worn by Sikhs. After the ceremony of prayers and hymns at the Gurdwara, fruit and Karah Parshad (a mixture of flour, milk, ghee and sugar) are shared out, followed by a vegetarian meal in an adjoining room called the Langar.

Learning objective: to find out about the cultures and beliefs of others.

What you need

Gold backing paper; paint; white card; black wool; foil; coloured fabric; white paper; information books about the Sikh religion such as *My Sikh Faith* by Kanwaljit Kaur-Singh (*Red Rainbows* series, Evans Brothers) or *My Sikh Life* by Kanwaljit Kaur-Singh (*Everyday Religion* series, Wayland); children's uniforms from home such as Brownie or Cub uniforms.

What to do

Share the information books with the children. Notice the clothing worn in the books and find examples of the five Ks. Tell the children that you are going to make a display which shows clothes worn by Sikh people, and include the five Ks.

Cover the display board with gold backing paper. Lay a large sheet of white paper on the floor and draw around a child, then cut out the outline. Encourage the children to paint the outline using appropriate skin tones. When the outline is dry, let the children paint in the facial features and stick on black wool hair and beard (Kesh).

Cut fabric to form a turban, white shorts (Kachera) and shirt and attach to the figure. Let the children add red fabric scraps to decorate the clothes. Add a white sash and belt. Cut the shape of a bracelet (Kara), short sword (Kirpan) and hair comb (Kangha) from foil. Attach the Kara to the figure's right wrist, the Kirpan to his left hand and the Kangha to the turban. When the figure is complete, attach it to the display board.

Add a title to your display and work together to make information cards for each of the five Ks. Display these around the figure together with pictures of each item, made by the children.

Cover a table with red fabric and display items brought in by the children, for example, a Brownie uniform, a special badge, a scarf, a hat, a nursery sweatshirt and so on.

Talk about

● Discuss special clothes. Do the children know anyone who wears a uniform?

Using the display

Personal, social and emotional development

● Use information books to look at pictures of Sikh women wearing saris. Invite a member of the Sikh community to show the children how a sari is worn.
● Talk about the 'Kangha' and the importance of caring for hair. Invite the children to wash a doll's hair with shampoo and to comb it.
● Discuss how special clothing can be used for protection. Look at protective helmets, gloves, overalls and so on.

Communication, language and literacy

● Introduce uniforms into role-play. Make your own tabard versions for simplicity.
● Explore the letter 'k'. Have a '"k" table' with objects starting with 'k' and include plastic, foam, wood and cardboard letters.

Mathematical development

● Collect together sets of five objects. Encourage the children to put sets of five into hoops, for example, five plastic farm animals, five teddies and so on.
● Sing number rhymes such as 'Five Currant Buns in a Baker's Shop' or 'Five Little Ducks Went Swimming One Day' from *This Little Puffin...* compiled by Elizabeth Matterson (Puffin Books).

Creative development

● Use malleable materials and modelling tools to make a model of something that is special to your setting, such as a symbol.

● Talk about the meaning and importance of the five 'K' words.

Home links

● Ask parents and other family members to visit your setting and show the children any special clothing or uniforms that they wear.
● Invite parents to send in objects for the '"k" table' (see 'Communication, language and literacy' above).

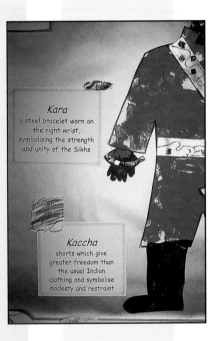

Kara
a steel bracelet worn on the right wrist, symbolising the strength and unity of the Sikhs

Kaccha
shorts which give greater freedom than the usual Indian clothing and symbolise modesty and restraint

Pesach

Pesach, or Passover, is an eight-day Jewish family festival of thanksgiving that is celebrated in spring. Jews remember how the ten plagues sent by God passed over their houses and into the houses of Egyptians. They also remember how, through Moses, God led them away from the bitterness of slavery by parting the waters of the Red Sea, to the sweetness of freedom in the promised land.

Before the festival begins, the family home is cleaned and, on the first night, a family meal called 'Seder' is served.

Various symbolic foods are served at the meal, including roast lamb; a roast egg (symbolising new life); maror, a bitter herb to remind them of the bitterness of slavery; and haroset, a fruit-and-nut sweet to remind them of the sweetness of freedom.

During the meal, the father of the family tells the story of how Moses parted the Red Sea to guide the Jews to freedom. After the meal, there is a blessing (Kiddush), prayers and hymns.

Learning objective: to listen with enjoyment and respond to favourite stories.

What you need

The Usborne Children's Bible retold by Heather Amery (Usborne Publishing); white and pale blue paper; red tissue, crêpe and sugar paper; paints in various colours; sponges; paintbrushes; painting paper; collage materials; fabric scraps; scissors; Moses basket (or one made by the children using a cardboard box and strips of paper); doll; blue fabric; bulrush plants or grasses in pots.

What to do

Begin by sharing stories about Moses' life from *The Usborne Children's Bible*. Talk about the stories and discuss the illustrations. Ask the children to help you make a display which shows Moses leading the Hebrews through the Red Sea.

Cover the display board with pale blue paper, sponge-painted to give texture, and add a border. Paint and cut out a bright sun, then mount it in one corner. Provide outlines of figures, and invite the children to use collage materials to represent Moses and some of his followers. Mount the finished figures towards the top of the display board.

Invite the children to help make the 'Red Sea'. Carefully cut strips of red sugar, tissue and crêpe paper into wavy shapes, and layer these across the bottom of the board to represent the sea. Provide paper and paint in a variety of bright colours and ask the children to paint colourful patterned fish. When the fish shapes are dry, cut them out and add them to the display to make them look like they are swimming in the sea.

In front of the display, arrange a table or display surface covered with blue fabric. Display the bulrush plants or grasses and place a doll in a Moses basket or decorated cardboard box.

Talk about
● Discuss the preparations for the festival of Pesach. How can the children help to spring-clean at home?
● Talk about the children's experiences of the sea. Reinforce the dangers of water.

Home links
● Encourage a family member to come and tell a favourite story to the children.

● Make up a story using the children's ideas. Create your own big book and add this to your display.
● Dramatize the stories of Moses in the bulrushes and the parting of the Red Sea.

Using the display
Personal, social and emotional development
● Talk about the special meal (Seder) and make comparisons with other special festival meals that the children enjoy. Encourage them to tell the group how they feel as they anticipate special events.
● Talk about how Moses' mother might have felt when she left him in the bulrushes. Be sensitive to individual circumstances.

Communication, language and literacy
● Discuss with the children the storytelling tradition after the Pesach meal. Show them a picture of the Haggadah, which tells the story of how Moses delivered his people from slavery, and retell a favourite story together.

Mathematical development
● Discuss the tradition of the youngest child at the Pesach meal being chosen to answer four important questions from the Haggadah. Talk about oldest and youngest members of the children's families.
● Make sequencing cards based on a favourite story and encourage the children to arrange them in order.

Knowledge and understanding of the world
● Make comparisons between different types of breads from other countries, such as baguettes, ciabatta and naan. Tell the children about leavened bread and the story of the people leaving their homes in a hurry, before the bread had time to rise.
● Do a survey to find out what the children's favourite breads are.

THEMES ON DISPLAY
for early years

Mother's Day

Mothering Sunday originated as a Christian celebration when people would take offerings to the mother church of the parish. It is celebrated on the fourth Sunday in Lent and is the one day when people can break their fast to celebrate. Servants were allowed to take the day off and visit their own mothers offering gifts of flowers and cakes.

Nowadays, children send cards and gifts to their mothers to express thanks for all that they do. But it is not only a day for mothers – it is also for grandmothers, foster mothers, stepmothers and female guardians.

Learning objectives: to encourage children to develop an appreciation of those who care for them; to raise awareness of how they can help others.

What you need
Coloured backing paper; contrasting border; heart-shaped sponges; painting paper; paints; crayons; coloured card; coloured tissue paper; art straws; sticky tape; glue; vase; bright fabric; netting; ribbons; pot-pourri; scissors.

What to do
Cover the display board with bright backing paper. Invite the children to think about all the things that their mummies

or other carers do for them. How can they show that they care on Mother's Day? They might help by tidying their room or laying the table. Talk about Mother's Day presents, such as chocolates or flowers. Explain that you are going to make a display which shows different ways in which the children can show their mummies that they care.

Provide paper, crayons and paints and ask the children to paint or draw pictures of themselves being helpful. Mount these on contrasting paper and display them on the board. Invite each child to write a short sentence describing their picture, or scribe for them, then mount these sentences alongside the pictures. Encourage the children to print pink hearts onto strips of paper to make a border for the display.

Place a table covered with bright fabric in front of the display. Invite the children to make Mother's Day cards using tissue paper discs and coloured card. Arrange these on and around the table. Make flowers by taping scrunched-up discs of coloured tissue paper to art straws. Display these in a colourful vase.

Make pot-pourri gift bags using discs of net and ribbon. Place some pot-pourri in the centre of each disc of netting and gather up the edges before securing with a ribbon. Complete your display with an appropriate heading.

Talk about
● Talk about special people who care for the children such as stepmothers, foster mothers and grandmothers. Be sensitive to family circumstances. Ask the children to think about how these special people care for them.

Home links
● Let the children take home their cards and presents just before Mother's Day.
● Invite mothers or female carers to a party and present them with the cards and presents. Enjoy home-made cakes, and sing songs.

Using the display
Personal, social and emotional development
● Take a photograph of each child and mount it on thick card. Ask the children to decorate around it with collage scraps of glitter and sequins, then laminate for protection. Display the photographs and discuss common features and ways in which we are different. Present them to mothers at the end of the week as a surprise gift.

Communication, language and literacy
● Think about all the special words that describe mothers, such as happy, friendly, loving and so on.
● Ask the children to help you make a list of ways that they can help at home.
● Make a big book about mothers. Encourage the children to draw pictures of the things that their mothers do, then help them to write captions under their drawings. Hang the book alongside the wall display.
● Write and illustrate invitations to your Mother's Day party celebration. Let the

children decide on the wording and have a go at the writing, according to their ability.

Knowledge and understanding of the world
● Bake some cakes to share when mothers visit. Talk about the changes that happen as the ingredients are mixed and cooked.

Creative development
● Try different techniques to make Mother's Day cards. Dry some flowers, leaves and grasses and stick them to card; make flowers from tissue paper discs, stick several on top of each other and scrunch them slightly to form petals. Draw pictures using glue and sprinkle on glitter.
● Make a present by sticking plastic straws into a clay ball and allowing the clay to harden. Paint it green and glue tissue discs to the straws to represent flowers in a clump of grass.

Naw-Ruz

Naw-Ruz is the Iranian celebration of New Year, lasting 13 days and coinciding with the spring Equinox when day and night are of equal length. A week before New Year, Iranians clean their homes and the first few days of Naw-Ruz are spent visiting family and friends to exchange gifts and enjoy a feast, which includes rice, fruit, olives, smoked fish and bread. On the last day of the celebrations, people leave their homes to visit parks and spend the day with nature.

A major part of the new year ritual is the setting of a table with seven specific food items all beginning with the Persian letter 's'. Among the things displayed on the table are wheat and barley to represent new growth, fish, water (it is believed that the fish turns over in the water when the new year begins), vinegar and lit candles to represent fire.

On the same day, the older Persian religion, Zoroastrianism, celebrates the festival of No-Rooz, when all activities are done in honour of fire, the symbol of truth.

Learning objective: to become familiar with letters by their sound and shape.

What you need
Pale backing paper; neutral sugar paper; wool; paints in various colours; foil; red Cellophane; glue; collage materials; patterned cloth; small bowls; tray; rice; olives; garlic; eggs; apples; grains; candles in holders; bulbs; grain seedlings; plants; information books about new year and new life; goldfish in a bowl; table; fabric.

What to do
Cover the display board with pale backing paper. Cut the shapes of a table and four chairs from neutral sugar paper and invite the children to paint them brown. When they are dry, mount them on the board. Draw the outlines of four people, as if seated on the chairs, and let the children add clothes and facial features using paints and collage materials. When dry, glue on wool to represent hair.

Remind the children of the foods associated with the festival. Ask them to make a collage of pictures of plates and bowls full of festival food such as a foil fish, painted black olives and rice. Cut around the outlines and add the pictures to the table.

Ask the children to make handprints using red and yellow paint. When dry, cut out and mount around the display to make a border of 'flames'. Paint candles with red foil or Cellophane flames and stick them to the bottom of the display. Cut out goldfish bowl shapes and help the children to cut foil fish outlines to stick inside the bowls. Arrange these between the candles.

Make a heading saying 'Happy Iranian New Year!' to attach above the display. Make smaller labels for key words such as 'goldfish', 'candles', 'summer' and 'winter' to stick around the display. Add some information text explaining the background to the festival.

In front of the display, arrange a low table covered with fabric. Display Iranian food beginning with the Persian letter 's' in small bowls on a tray (for example, rice, olives, garlic, apples, grains and eggs). Place bulbs, plants and grain seedlings around the tray to symbolize new life. Display candles in holders and a selection of information books. If you have a goldfish in a bowl, include this.

Talk about
● Discuss the dangers of fire.

Home links
● Do any of the children have a pet goldfish? Encourage them to tell the group how they have to look after it. Ask parents to send in photographs of family pets, and create a group display.
● Ask parents to supply items beginning with the letter 's' for an interest table.

Using the display
Personal, social and emotional development
● Consider the needs of the goldfish. Let the children share the responsibility for feeding it and helping to change the water.

Communication, language and literacy
● Have an '"s" day'. Do activities, play games and sing songs beginning with 's', and have sandwiches, satsumas and sultanas at snack time!
● Give each child a copy of the 'Starting with "s"' photocopiable sheet on page 75. Invite them to identify, name and colour in the items that begin with the letter 's'.

Knowledge and understanding of the world
● Observe how a goldfish swims. How does it eat and breathe?
● Cook some rice and compare the texture with the uncooked rice from your display.

Physical development
● Make piles of beanbags to represent small bonfires and jump over them.

olives

THEMES ON DISPLAY
for early years

Easter bonnets

Learning objective: to select and use a variety of resources and equipment.

What you need
Paper plates; margarine tubs; ribbons; glue; tissue and crêpe paper; coloured feathers; magazine pictures of flowers and fruit; scissors; paint; straw hats; bright fabric.

What to do
Talk about the tradition of wearing decorated bonnets at Easter. Tell the children that they are going to make their own bonnets.

Give each child a paper plate and invite them to paint it using bright colours. Once dry, stick an upside-down margarine tub onto each plate. Cut a hole in the centre of each plate, and cut strips from the hole to the edge of the tub. Fold and glue these to the inside edge of the tub to reinforce the join. Invite the children to cut pictures of flowers and fruit from magazines to decorate their bonnets, and add tissue and crêpe paper. Attach ribbons to the inside of each bonnet so that they can be secured under the children's chins.

Display the bonnets on a fabric-covered table. Label each with details of the designer and the things that they used to make their bonnet. Extend the display by inviting the children to decorate straw hats with feathers and other collage materials.

Talk about
● Discuss the pictures on the bonnets. What other images could the children include to represent new life?
● Talk about Easter parades. Let the children wear their bonnets as they parade around the room.

Home links
● Ask parents to donate old hats for the children to decorate, and items for decorating them, such as artificial flowers and ribbon.

Further table display ideas
● Place resources to make Easter nests on a table. Include boxes, straw and tissue paper. Let the children add a small chocolate or sugar egg to their nest before taking them home.
● Make an 'Egg head' display table. Let the children decorate empty egg shells to look like funny faces. Fill the eggshells with cotton wool and sprinkle on cress seeds, then water liberally and wait for the cress 'hair' to grow!
● Create a 'New life' table with seedlings, bulbs and twigs arranged on fake grass.

Summer festivals

May Day

May Day has been celebrated for many years, and the first Monday in May is now a national holiday. Many years ago, villagers would select a young tall tree as a maypole, stripping off its lower branches and leaving the higher ones to represent new life. People decorated the tree with ribbons and flower garlands, and danced around it. A young girl from the village was chosen as the May queen. Maypoles are still created in some towns and the May queen travels on a flower-covered lorry as part of a May Day procession.

Learning objective: to express ideas, thoughts and feelings through music, dance and play.

What you need
Bright backing paper; paints; painting paper; ribbons or crêpe paper; large cardboard tube; drawing pins; glue; coloured tissue paper; floral table-cloth; vases of flowers; art straws; pencil or dowelling; thin ribbons; sticky tape; clay; small-world figures.

What to do
Cover a display board with bright backing paper. Create a maypole by covering a cardboard tube with contrasting strips of crêpe paper, then attach to the board. Ask the children to paint pictures of themselves dancing and attach these to the board, linking them to the maypole with the crêpe paper or ribbons. Give the figures flower garlands made from coloured tissue paper. Make colourful flowers to frame the display by gluing scrunched-up tissue paper to coloured sugar paper.

Cover a table with floral fabric. Involve the children in making May Day cards, 'flowers' and hats. Display these on the table, with vases of flowers.

On another table, create a small-world maypole dancing display. Secure a pencil in a lump of clay, and tape thin, coloured ribbons to the top of the pencil. Display this in the centre of the table and attach the ends of the ribbons to small-world figures.

Talk about
● Discuss the clothes worn by the May queen. Talk about the children's favourite party outfits.
● Talk about different types of dancing, such as Morris or country dancing.

Home links
● Make a maypole using a secure post and invite parents to watch the children doing a May Day dance.

The colourful festivals that take place during the summer months are the focus for this series of displays. Ideas include a vibrant Chinese Dragon Boat display and a rainy weather picture based on the festival of St Swithun's Day.

THEMES ON DISPLAY
for early years

Wesak

Wesak is celebrated by Buddhists in the month of Visakha, which is usually in May or June. It is the time when they remember the birth, enlightenment and death of Buddha which all happened on the same day in different years. The story is about Prince Siddattha who lived a protected life in his palace. One day he decided to venture beyond the palace and discovered that many people were sick, old and poor. He gave up his own wealth and, as Buddha, set out to help others.

Today, Buddhists decorate their homes and temples with lanterns and flowers, incense sticks and candles and give gifts to the poor during Wesak. Flowers are placed in front of statues of Buddha and sermons tell of the teachings of Buddha. Sometimes, as a symbol of compassion, animals, birds and fish, normally held in captivity, are set free by monks.

Learning objective: to understand the importance of showing kindness to others and care and concern towards animals.

What you need

Backing paper in two contrasting colours; potatoes; paints; paper; ribbon; card; thick grey paint; scrubbing brushes; scourers; sequins; glue; photographs of children's pets; crayons; clay; coloured Cellophane; coloured fabric; table.

What to do

Cover your display board with pale backing paper. Cut the outline of an elephant from card and ask the children to paint it with thick grey paint. Before the paint dries, ask the children to brush over it with scrubbing brushes and plastic scourers to create the texture of elephant skin. Cut a piece of fabric to shape and decorate it with sequins before attaching it to the elephant's back. Paint the elephant's eye. Mount the completed elephant on bright backing paper before attaching to the display board.

Ask the children to make a border for the display. Provide them with potato halves cut into the shape of flowers, and let them use bright paint to print flowers. When dry, cut out the individual prints and arrange in clusters around the elephant to make flower garlands.

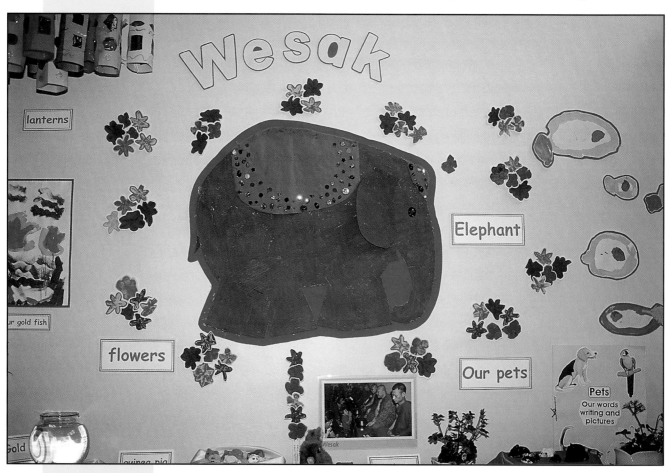

Share the photographs of the children's pets, and encourage them to create drawings and paintings to make a big book. Add this to the display and fix a title across the top. Make lanterns to suspend from the ceiling. Show the children how to carefully cut holes in folded card and stick coloured Cellophane behind the holes to create a stained-glass effect.

In front of the display, place a table covered with colourful fabric. Help the children to make model animals, birds and fish with clay. Paint the models and display them on the table.

Talk about
● Discuss the importance of sharing and taking turns.
● Talk about the need to handle animals with care and respect.

Home links
● Ask parents to bring in a pet and talk about how they care for it. (**NB** Follow your policy for allowing animals into your setting.)
● Ask for donations of different types of flowering plants, and cut flowers to display during Wesak.
● Copy the 'Kindness certificate' photocopiable sheet on page 76. Fill these certificates in when individuals have done kind deeds, and let them take the sheet home to share with their families.

Using the display
Personal, social and emotional development
● Tell the story of Prince Siddattha and how he gave up his wealth to help those less fortunate than him. Talk about the people who are kind to the children. Make a list of ways that the children could be kind to others.
● Make a rota for caring for a nursery pet. Discuss its needs.
● Talk about the needs of wild animals, such as food, water and shelter. What do animals eat? Where do they find shelter? Emphasize the need to leave wildlife undisturbed.
● Together, devise a list of rules for appropriate behaviour in your setting. Display these in a prominent place and refer to them regularly.

Communication, language and literacy
● Gather together at the start of the session to discuss ways that the

children can help one another that day. Meet together at the end of the session to talk about the kindness that they have experienced.

Physical development
● Talk about how animals feel when they are free in their natural habitat. Pretend to fly like birds, swim like fish and run like wild animals.

Creative development
● Talk about how the monks sometimes set the captured birds and fish free to remember the love that Buddha had for all living things, then paint pictures of birds, animals and fish.
● Make colourful lanterns and garlands to decorate your home corner.
● Make collage pictures of flowers using brightly-coloured tissue, Cellophane and foil scraps.
● Make observational drawings of the flowers and plants brought in by parents and carers.

Dragon Boat Festival

The Dragon Boat Festival is celebrated during the dragon month of the Chinese calendar, which is around June. The Chinese remember Ch'u Yuen who, long ago, tried to save the poor people from paying heavy taxes to the Emperor. When he pleaded with the Emperor to be more lenient, the Emperor refused, so Ch'u Yuen decided to commit suicide by throwing himself into a lake to draw attention to the bad government. The poor people took a boat into the lake. They made loud noises and threw rice wrapped in bamboo leaves into the water to keep the dragons and demons at bay while they tried to find Ch'u Yuen, without success.

Today, Chinese people have races in boats shaped like dragons. Rice dumplings are traditionally made from sticky rice, meat, beans and nuts wrapped in bamboo leaves. The festival also celebrates water, and the end of winter leading to the start of summer. People clean their houses and remember how important water and rain are for the success of their harvest.

Learning objective: to move confidently, showing control and coordination.

What you need
White frieze paper; thin card in two colours; blue and white paints; sponges; cardboard combs; recycled collage materials; glue; coloured tissue paper and Cellophane; card; coloured foil; rice; paints; books, artefacts and models relating to the festival.

What to do
Lay a sheet of paper the size of the display area on the floor. Help the children to sponge-paint the top half with light blue paint to create the sky. Use thick darker blue paint on the bottom half to create the sea. Create waves with cardboard combs and add white paint for foam. When dry, mount on the display board.

FESTIVALS

Cut the outlines of two large dragon boats from coloured card. Show the children the recycled pots, tissue, foil and Cellophane, and encourage them to decorate the boats with these. Challenge them to be as creative as possible, and ask them to make the boats really colourful. As you work, discuss features such as scales, eyes, teeth and hair, and let the children choose the most appropriate resources to create these effects. When complete, attach the two dragon boats on the display in the 'sea'. Make a border of foil fish shapes and scattered rice grains. Add the words 'Dragon Boat Festival' as a title for your display.

In front of your display, arrange models of dragon boats if available, books and other artefacts associated with the festival.

Talk about
● Discuss the story behind the festival.
● Talk about different types of races. Have the children ever watched a race, or maybe participated in one?

Home links
● Invite parents to help the children to make the colourful dragons for your display.
● Compile a list of the recycled materials that you will need to create the dragon boat models. Display this in your reception area, and ask parents to contribute items from home.

Using the display
Personal, social and emotional development
● Talk about dragons, including those in stories. Do they make the children feel frightened? Discuss how Chinese dragons bring good fortune and so are not considered to be frightening.

Mathematical development
● Have a dragon boat race in the water tray using numbered boats. Invite up to five children to decorate margarine tubs before numbering them. Place them in the water tray and use straws to blow them across the water. Which number comes first? Which comes second? Last?

Knowledge and understanding of the world
● Soak some rice in the water tray and cook some in water. Compare dry, soaked and cooked grains.

● Experiment with making dragon boats from plastic bottles. Which bottle shapes are most effective? Why?

Physical development
● Sit on the floor in small groups and pretend to have a 'dragon boat' race as you sing 'Row, Row, Row Your Boat'.
● Make a child-size dragon boat from large cardboard boxes and small chairs and let the children pretend to row it along together.

Creative development
● Explain how the Chinese people scared away the fish and dragons by making loud noises (there is no need to mention that Ch'u Yuen drowned). Use instruments to make a frightening noise, then try to make quiet sounds.
● Make dragon boats from recycled materials and paint them in bright colours. Display them on a blue cloth to represent water.

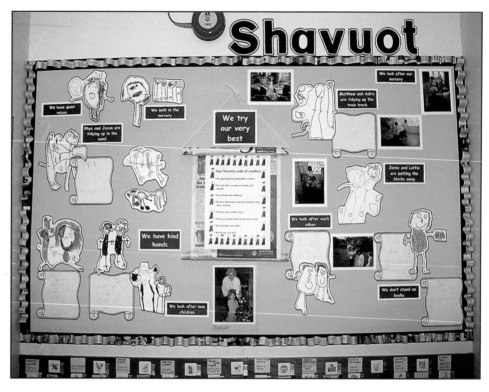

Shavuot

Shavuot takes place in May or June and is an ancient Jewish harvest festival. It takes place seven weeks after Pesach (Passover), marking the end of the barley festival and the beginning of the wheat festival. Jewish people remember Moses, and the many laws that were introduced during his life, including giving the first fruits of the harvest as an offering of thanks. They also remember how at this time of year, Moses was given the Ten Commandments, which are presented in the Jewish holy book – the Torah. Today, Jewish people decorate their synagogues with fruit, and dairy products and honey are eaten to remember that there was hardly any meat or fish during the time when the Jews were travelling through the wilderness with Moses to Israel (the land of milk and honey).

Learning objective: to become aware of the difference between right and wrong and the effects of actions upon others.

What you need
Yellow frieze paper; contrasting border paper; paints; crayons; newspaper; sticky tape; two long cardboard tubes; black and white paper; books about caring such as *Alfie Gives a Hand* by Shirley Hughes (Red Fox); fabric; card; pictures and posters of people helping others.

What to do
Cover the display board with yellow frieze paper and add an interesting border made by stapling strips of newspaper at intervals to give an undulating effect. Make a Torah scroll by rolling a large strip of newspaper around two long cardboard tubes. Stick the paper to the tubes, covering the ends with discs of card. Attach the 'Torah' to the centre of the display.

Talk about rules that are followed in your setting, such as picking up toys, being kind to each other and putting rubbish in the bin. Make a list of these rules, either written out in bold letters or word-processed. Attach this to the 'Torah' in the centre of the display. Ask the children to choose one of the rules and to paint or draw a picture of themselves carrying out that rule. Ask each child in turn to tell you what they are doing in their picture and then help them to write a short sentence, or scribe for them. When the pictures are complete, mount them on contrasting paper and display them on the board around the 'Torah' together with the children's writing. Add other pictures of people doing kind deeds. Add a heading to complete your display.

In front of the display, arrange books about caring for each other on a covered table.

Talk about
● Discuss the significance of the Torah.
● Look at the children's handwriting and compare it to the print of the newspaper that is on the display. Talk about how both pieces of text convey information.

Home links
● Tell carers that you have been thinking about rules. Ask them to encourage awareness of appropriate behaviour at home.
● Send home a children's newsletter with their own contributions and illustrations of current activities.
● Let the children share their achievements with their families by taking home a copy of the 'Kindness certificate' sheet on page 76 when they have carried out a kind deed. Fill in the child's name, describe their kind act, and sign and date the certificate.

We don't stand on books

Using the display
Personal, social and emotional development
● Talk about appropriate behaviour in your setting. Discuss actions that might cause discomfort to others, such as throwing sand. Visit each area in your setting together and compile a list of rules.

Communication, language and literacy
● Look at pictures of the Torah and talk about the shape of the scroll. Explain how scrolls were written and compare this with the children's books. Discuss changes in written communication, using examples such as typewritten letters, word-processed information and faxes.

Mathematical development
● Help to develop counting and number recognition by adding number rules at various activities. For example, add the outline of three children to the painting area together with a sign that says '3 children can paint here'.
● Moses received ten commandments. Together, choose the ten most important rules for your setting and make a numbered list.

Knowledge and understanding of the world
● Shavuot takes place at the end of the barley harvest and the beginning of the wheat harvest. Examine some grains of wheat and barley. Crush them and notice what happens. Discuss what needs to be done to the grains to turn them into flour or cereals, then investigate things that are made using the flour.
● Taste various wheat-based cereals and make comparisons between taste and texture. (**NB** Check for food allergies first.)

Creative development
● Paint colourful pictures of fruit and use them to decorate your setting.
● Create collages of pictures of flowers using fabric scraps, tissue or colourful wrapping paper.

THEMES ON DISPLAY
for early years

Raksha Bandhan

The festival of Raksha Bandhan takes place in July or August and is celebrated by Hindus and Sikhs. Raksha means 'to protect' and Bandhan means 'to tie'. Hindus remember the story of Indra, king of the lesser gods, whose wife was given a thread by the god Vishnu to tie around her husband's wrist to protect him in battle against the demon king, Bali. Indra won the battle and regained his kingdom. Nowadays, Raksha Bandhan is a day when sisters honour their brothers, and brothers promise to protect their sisters. Sisters make a 'rakhi' for their brothers. This is a band of coloured thread, which they tie around their brothers' wrists. They also mark their brothers' foreheads with red powder and pray that they will be protected from evil. The brothers then promise to protect their sisters.

Learning objective: to talk about, recognize and recreate patterns.

What you need
Colourful frieze paper; contrasting border paper; yellow paper; scissors; paints; crayons; tray; card; wool; felt-tipped pens; sequins; hole punch; coloured fabric; table; books such as *Children Just Like Me* by Barnabas and Anabel Kindersley (*Celebration!* series, Dorling Kindersley) and *Titch* by Pat Hutchins (Bodley Head).

What to do
Cover the display area with bright paper and add a contrasting border. Invite the children to participate in a discussion

about brothers and sisters, relatives of their age or special friends. Tell them that you are going to make a display about Raksha Bandhan and you would like them to paint a picture of themselves with their brother, sister, relative or friend. Provide plenty of time for the children to create their pictures. Then, when these are dry, mount them on bright paper before attaching them to the board.

Fold yellow paper into zigzags and help the children to cut paper-chain figures. Open the paper out to reveal the figures 'holding hands'. Attach these at intervals around the border, leaving them slightly raised to give a 3-D effect. Add a colourful title to complete your display.

Cover a table with coloured fabric. Write the children's names onto individual pieces of card and place these in a tray on the table. Display the items needed to make 'rakhi' bracelets such as wool, card, sequins, felt-tipped pens and a hole punch.

Talk about
● Discuss the story behind the festival or Raksha Bandhan. Talk about other special times that we give presents, such as birthdays, Christmas and so on.
● Talk about ways of showing that we care for one another.

Home links
● Ask parents to send in a few photographs of family groups, especially brothers and sisters, with a note about each of the subjects' names and ages. Discuss the photographs in turn, encouraging the children to offer additional information about the people in the pictures.
● Invite parents and carers to show photographs of their own brothers and sisters to their children. Encourage them to share their own childhood memories with their children.

Using the display
Personal, social and emotional development
● Talk about brothers and sisters. Take care to be sensitive to individual family circumstances, perhaps talking about special friends instead. How do the children demonstrate kindness to their brothers and sisters or special friends?
● Talk about the games that the children play with their siblings or friends at home. Discuss the importance of sharing toys and taking turns when playing together.

Mathematical development
● Ask the children to draw pictures of their families. Count the people in each family and display the pictures in groups – for example, families of four all together. Talk about the advantages of both small and large families.
● Read the story of *Titch* by Pat Hutchins and discuss Titch's place in the family. Encourage the children to use language such as 'older' and 'youngest' to describe their family.
● Give each child a copy of the 'Make your own rakhis' photocopiable sheet on page 77. Invite them to use bright

pens to create patterns in the rectangles. When they have completed each rectangle, ask them to choose their favourite one and help them to cut it out. Use a hole punch to make a hole in each end, then tie the strips around the children's wrists, securing with coloured thread.

Knowledge and understanding of the world
● Make a list of physical things that the children can do such as jumping, hopping and running. Discuss what younger brothers and sisters do. Talk about growing and learning new skills.

Creative development
● Look at photographs of brothers and sisters and talk about whether they have similar features. Paint pictures of them to display alongside the photographs.
● Invite the children to use the resources on the display table to make rakhis. Let them take these home to give to a brother, relative or friend.

St Swithun's Day

St Swithun became Bishop of
Winchester in 852AD and on 15 July,
we remember his story. He loved the
poor and tried to help them in any way
he could. He told them that he did not
wish to be buried inside the cathedral,
but outside under the rain where
everyone who came to worship,
including the poor people, could walk
over his grave. His wish was granted,
but within a few days, the monks
planned to move his body inside. When
they began to dig up his grave, it began
to rain and the harder they worked, the
more it rained. The monks decided to
leave the grave until the rain stopped. It
continued to rain for forty days until the
monks decided to leave St Swithun's
grave outside. People say that the rain
happened because St Swithun did not
want to be moved. It is said that if it
rains on St Swithun's day, then it will rain
for the next forty days.

*Learning objective: to listen with
enjoyment and respond to rhyming
words and syllables.*

What you need
Newspaper; pale blue frieze paper; neutral
sugar paper; blue paint; blue foil; dark blue
paper; fabric scraps; recycled collage
materials; glue; plastic bottles; scissors;
rainy day items such as umbrellas, hats,

wellington boots and so on; blue fabric; information books and story-books such as *In the Rain with Baby Duck* by Amy Hest (Walker Books) and *Rain and Shine* by Paul Rogers (Orchard Books).

What to do

Share the story of St Swithun with the children, then say some rainy day rhymes together, such as 'Doctor Foster' and 'Incy Wincy Spider'. Explain that you are going to make a rainy day display about the rhyme 'Doctor Foster'.

Cover a large area with newspaper and lay a large sheet of pale blue frieze paper on top. Invite the children to splatter blue paint onto the paper to look like rain. When the splatter-painted paper is dry, use it to cover the board. Ask a child to lie down on a sheet of neutral sugar paper, and draw around him or her to create the outline of Doctor Foster. Let the children use fabric scraps and collage materials to 'dress' the figure in appropriate clothing. Add facial features and details such as a hat and glasses. Provide a pre-cut umbrella outline and invite the children to decorate the individual sections using colourful fabric scraps. Attach the umbrella to the display so that Doctor Foster looks like he is carrying it.

Let the children paint rainy day pictures. Mount these on dark blue paper before arranging them around the board. Finish your display with a border of blue foil raindrops and a title.

Arrange a table in front of your display and cover it with blue fabric. Add the rainy day books and clothing. Together with the children, make rain gauges by marking measurements on cut-down plastic bottles and add these to the table.

Talk about

● Discuss the story behind St Swithun's Day. Do the children think it will really rain for forty days?
● Talk about rainy days. What do the children like and dislike about them?

Home links

● Ask parents to contribute rainy day items for the display.
● Send home a copy of the rhyme 'Doctor Foster' asking parents to share it with their children and take them for a walk on a rainy day.

Using the display
Communication, language and literacy

● Think of rain words such as 'splish', 'splash' and 'drip'. Write them on large card raindrops and suspend these in front of the display.
● Say the rhyme 'Doctor Foster' emphasizing the rhyming words 'rain' and 'again', 'Foster' and 'Gloucester'.

Mathematical development

● Make a simple rain gauge from a clear plastic bottle. Cut off the top and invert it into the rest of the bottle to form a funnel. Mark the side of the bottle in centimetres to ten. Look at the gauge regularly and discuss the amount of rain collected.

Knowledge and understanding of the world

● Draw around a puddle with white chalk. Go outside later in the day and draw around the puddle again. What has happened?
● Look closely at different umbrellas and talk about how they work.
● Explore displacement: mark a point midway up the side of a transparent container with a thick elastic band, fill it with water to that point, then drop pebbles in and watch the water rise.

Physical development

● Encourage the children to dress in waterproof clothes and wellington boots on a rainy day, and to enjoy splashing in puddles.

Creative development

● Cover a large sheet of paper with a thin coat of water, which has been coloured with a drop of blue colouring. Invite the children to drop 'rain drops' of dark blue paint onto the paper and to watch them spread.

THEMES ON DISPLAY
for early years

World Environment Day

Learning objective: to encourage an awareness of the natural environment.

World Environment Day is celebrated on 5 June and is a time when nations unite to become aware of issues relating to our environment. The day was established in 1972, marking the Stockholm Conference on the Human Environment. On Environment Day, people consider how they can protect their environment and they celebrate in many ways, for example, by having bicycle parades, tree-planting ceremonies, recycling events or by cleaning up towns and cities.

Every year, a different city is chosen by UNEP (United Nations Environment Programme) to be the main venue for the international celebrations. At the end of the main event, UNEP presents awards to environmentalists from all over the world who have made outstanding contributions to protecting our environment.

What you need
Neutral sugar paper or newspaper; household junk items made from different materials including metal, plastic and paper; string; card; paper plate; glue; grey paper; bubble wrap; boxes; bright wallpaper.

What to do
Investigate the household junk items with the children, and explain that you are going to recycle the items to create a display. Back the display board with neutral paper or newspaper. Cut the rough outline of a person from card, and lay it on the table. Invite the children to create a 'junk man' by selecting appropriate resources from your household junk selection and gluing them onto the outline. Give your 'junk man' a happy face, made by adding junk material and fabric scraps to a large paper plate. Add string or wool to represent hair.

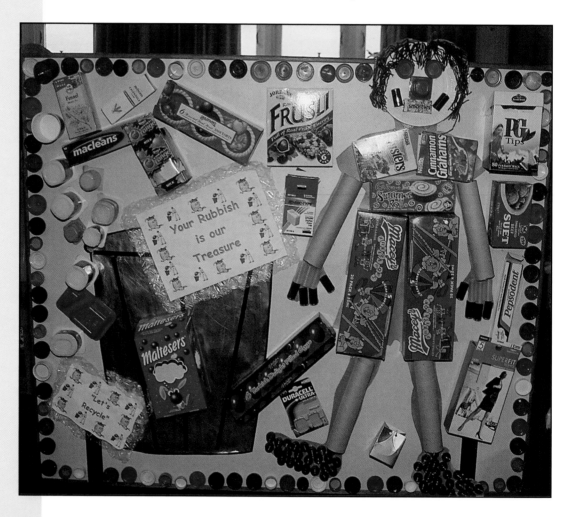

Attach the 'junk man' to the display. Cut the outline of a large bin from grey paper and mount it on the board. Affix a selection of junk items around the figure and the bin and add a title that says 'Your rubbish is our treasure'. Choose smaller junk items such as foil pie or cake cases to make a colourful border for your display.

Cover a table with bright wallpaper and place it near to the display. Arrange three boxes on the table: one covered in foil, one in bubble wrap and another in wallpaper. Label each box clearly: 'Metallic objects', 'Plastic' and 'Paper and card'. Invite the children to sort any junk items that you collect into the correct boxes.

Talk about
● Discuss the importance of caring for the environment. Talk about ways that the children can help, for example, by not dropping litter and not picking wild flowers from trees and plants.
● Why is it important to recycle used items? Think about the consequences of using too many of the Earth's resources and of creating too much rubbish.

Home links
● Ask parents and carers to contribute clean, empty containers and packaging for your display.
● Ask parents and carers to take their children to visit a bottle bank and to recycle cans and newspapers.
● Invite a parent or carer to talk about gardening and how they care for the things that they grow.

Using the display
Personal, social and emotional development
● Organize a rota for tidying your setting. Discuss the importance of keeping things in the correct places and putting them back after use. Ensure that storage containers are clearly labelled and easily accessible to encourage this.
● Plant seeds in pots and encourage the children to tend to them regularly.

Communication, language and literacy
● Sing rhymes about wildlife such as 'Five Little Speckled Frogs' or 'Five Little Ducks' and discuss their needs and habitats.

Knowledge and understanding of the world
● Find out more about UNEP by visiting the website: www.unep.org
● Talk about the importance of clean water. Mix some soil in clear water and watch it settle. Create a filter in a sieve by placing a coffee filter in the bottom and then a layer of sand, gravel and finally stones. Pour in the dirty water and talk about what happens. Stress that the children must not drink the water even though it looks clear.
● Recreate a forest habitat using a shallow tray and some compost. Add model trees, twigs and plastic animals and let the children play freely. Discuss the needs of the animals as the children play.

Physical development
● Try to become involved in local tree- or bulb-planting initiatives.
● Go for a walk and talk about where to put rubbish. Can you see any litter bins? Is there much rubbish on the ground? What happens to the rubbish when the bins are collected?

Creative development
● Look closely at a tree and make a 3-D tree from cardboard tubes or a large branch. Add paper leaves, straw nests, model birds and toy wildlife. Talk about the importance of trees for shelter, timber and paper.

THEMES ON DISPLAY
for early years

Japanese Children's Day

Japanese Children's Day, or Kodomono-hi, is celebrated on 5 May. Originally, this festival honoured the boys in the family, so the traditions associated with the day symbolize the qualities of strength and determination.

On Japanese Children's Day, kites and streamers are flown on long bamboo poles. Kites are made in the shape of carp, a fish which shows great strength and determination by swimming upstream against strong currents, jumping high in the water over obstacles. Each pole has a kite for the father, mother and each son attached to it. During the festival, Japanese people wear traditional dress and eat special rice cakes or 'chimaki' wrapped in oak or bamboo leaves. Iris leaves, symbolizing the swords of the warriors, are dropped into the bath water of boys to protect them from illness and to make them strong.

Learning objective: to look closely at the parts of a flower and record what they see through observational drawings.

What you need
Vase of irises; paper of different colours and sizes; magnifying glasses; felt-tipped pens; pencils.

What to do
Encourage the children to work at the display table in small groups. Invite them to study the irises carefully using the magnifying glasses. Talk about the colours and shapes that they can see. Let them choose appropriately-coloured pens or pencils to make detailed drawings of the irises.

Talk about
● Discuss the significance of the carp. Explain that the strength, bravery and determination of the carp are qualities that Japanese people encourage in their sons.
● Talk about the importance of trying hard in whatever we do.

Home links
● Make kites for the children to take home and fly.

Further table display ideas
● Have a kite-making table with colourful recycled materials and appropriate tools for children to explore on their own.
● Set up a fish-colouring table. Include a selection of pre-cut fish shapes, and supply card, paper, tissue and different mark-making tools. Provide information books such as *Children Just Like Me* by Barnabas and Anabel Kindersley (*Celebration!* series, Dorling Kindersley) and pictures for the children to refer to.

Autumn festivals

Harvest around the world

Harvest is a festival celebrated by people in many countries around the world. Christians in Britain celebrate Harvest during September and October. They display food in church and hold Harvest thanksgiving services. Afterwards, the food is often distributed to elderly members of the community. All around the world, people celebrate Harvest in a similar way, gathering food from their own cultures.

Learning objective: to raise awareness of the world beyond the children's own experiences.

What you need
Window area with window sill; pale and dark blue backing paper; world map; paints; fruit and vegetables from other countries, for example, mangoes from Brazil, kiwi fruit and limes from Australia, and satsumas and oranges from Africa (ask parents and carers for contributions); white paper; string or wool; map pins; sticky tape; sponge cut into fruit and vegetable shapes; pictures of flags from different countries.

What to do
This display looks most effective when created in a window area. Mount the pale blue paper on the window, and cover the area below with dark blue paper. Attach a map of the world to the dark blue paper and add the heading 'Harvest around the world'. Display the products, fruit and vegetables on the window sill above the map of the world. Label each product with its

country of origin. Ask the children to help you find each country on the map, then use string or wool to link the product to the corresponding country on the map. Make a border by sponge-printing fruit and vegetable shapes onto strips of white paper. Ask each child to choose a flag from a foreign country and to paint it. Place all the children's flags around the display, or as a separate display nearby. Label each flag with its country name.

Talk about
● Talk about the names of the products and the children's experiences of them.
● Discuss why we say 'thank you' at harvest time for the food that we eat.

Home links
● Ask parents and carers to look at the words on food packaging with their children and discuss where the products come from.

New years, new moons and harvest are the themes behind the festivals in this chapter. Ideas include a beautiful Chinese Moon Festival display, a colourful patterned peacock for Divali, and an interactive role-play display for Sukkot.

Ethiopian New Year

On 11 September, Rastafarians world-wide celebrate their New Year. It is a time when Rastafarian families gather together to worship as well as sing, dance and eat good food. Strict Rastafarians eat only natural or organic food and many are vegetarians. They like to wear traditional African clothes which are usually simple in style and are made in the colours of the Ethiopian flag: red, golden yellow and green. White clothes are worn on most holy days.

Learning objective: to create and copy simple patterns.

What you need

Black sugar paper; gold paper; white sheet; red, green, yellow and black paints; strips of white paper; strips of red, green and yellow paper (2cm x 15cm); glue; pencils; string; kitchen-roll tubes; elastic bands; potato and sponge cut into discs and crescents; empty dried baby-milk tins; thick plastic; PVA glue; two brightly-coloured table-cloths; exotic fruit and vegetables; white paper; scrap fabric; felt-tipped pens; crayons.

What to do

Back the display board with gold paper. Draw around three children onto black sugar paper and cut out the outlines. Ask the children to use paint or cut-out paper shapes to make happy faces, and attach the figures to the display.

THEMES ON DISPLAY for early years

Invite the children to dip round and crescent-shaped sponge and potato pieces in red, green, yellow and black paints, and to print the shapes onto a white sheet. Once dry, cut the sheet to size and staple these simple 'outfits' to the figures. Keep the spare material for later.

Ask the children to make bead necklaces. Roll strips of red, green and yellow paper tightly around a pencil and tape the end to make a bead. Thread the beads onto lengths of string in repeating patterns, then attach them to the display around the figures' necks. Cut out pieces of fabric to make scarves, or knitted hats which are known as 'tams' and worn by Rastafarians.

Show the children how to make model drums. Paint kitchen-roll tubes with red, green or yellow paint. When dry, cut in half to create small 'drum' shapes. Cut small discs from the printed fabric and secure over the ends of the 'drums' with elastic bands. Alternatively, mix one part paint with two parts PVA glue, and paint designs onto empty dried baby-milk tins. When dry, cover the ends of each tin with a disc of thick plastic secured with a large elastic band.

Create paper flags using red, green and yellow pens or paint, and stick them around the display. Add a large title to complete the display. Arrange and label examples of tropical fruit and vegetables on a table covered with a bright table-cloth, together with the children's home-made drums.

Talk about
● Discuss the unusual fruit on display. What do they feel like? Do the children like the smell?
● Talk about the clothes that the figures are wearing.

Home links
● Ask parents to make simple robes from sheeting, for the children to wear during role-play.
● Ask for suitable 'drum' containers.

tout

pineapple

Using the display
Personal, social and emotional development
● Ask the children to look at the Rastafarian hair-style and to make comparisons with their own hair-styles. Talk about how we care for our hair.
● Discuss the Rastafarian diet. What do the children like to eat?

Mathematical development
● Invite the children to copy single repeating patterns using paint, felt-tipped pens and crayons.
● Let the children make their own paper necklaces to wear. Experiment with different repeating patterns.

Knowledge and understanding of the world
● Pass around some mangoes and talk about their shape and colour. Cut them into slices and taste them. Discuss the flavour and texture.
● Pass around a yam and encourage the children to talk about its colour and shape. Feel it and smell it. Peel and slice two or three yams. Cook them, allow them to cool and ask the children to mash them with forks and a masher. Compare the raw and cooked yams.

Physical development
● Have a marching band with the home-made drums. Play some reggae music and march up and down with the drums or wave home-made Ethiopian flags. Suitable music is available from Knock on Wood, tel: 01423-712712; try their 'The Rough Guide to Reggae Music' cassette.

Creative development
● Make simple tabards for dolls in your setting to wear. Ask the children to print pieces of cotton fabric using red, green and yellow paints. When this is dry, sew the sides of the fabric together using wool and large blunt needles.

THEMES ON DISPLAY
for early years

Chinese Moon Festival

Learning objective: to find out and observe changes in the natural world associated with the passing of time.

Zhongqui Jie, the Mid-Autumn or Moon Festival, is held on the day before the full moon around the end of September. It is a major Chinese festival where incense is burned and offerings of fruit and moon cakes are made to the moon goddess and to the hare who lives on the moon. The festival celebrates an ancient legend about a wicked emperor who was given a potion that could give him immortality. His wife, Chang Er, drank the potion to save the Chinese people. When her husband tried to kill her, she flew up to the moon where she has lived ever since.

During the festival, Chinese people sit outside in the evening or take their children to high vantage points so that they can see the moon clearly. There are lion dances and lantern parades in the streets. The lanterns are made in shapes of traditional fish and animals. Special food is eaten, including moon-shaped fruit, sweet sticky rice and moon cakes, and is served on a table facing the moon.

What you need
Silver foil; blown vinyl wallpaper; black and blue paper; white card; paint; glue; moon-shaped fruit (for example oranges, melon slices and bananas); yellow fabric; bowls; balloons; plastic pots and other circular objects; newspaper; paste.

What to do
Back the wall in black paper to represent the night sky. Cut out a full moon, half-moon and crescent moon from white card and cover these in PVA glue. Help the children to press a piece of foil on top of each shape and gently crumple it to create the impression of the moon's irregular surface. Stick the moons in sequence across the centre of the board. Create a border of small moon shapes in the different phases, cut from blown vinyl wallpaper.

Invite the children to use different techniques to create moon pictures. Provide circular pieces of black and blue paper and encourage the group to print

circles using the ends of plastic pots and other circular objects; to create a stippling effect using large paintbrushes; and to use sponges to blend colours. Mount the pictures on dark blue paper before arranging them around the silvery moons.

Create a 3-D moon to hang in front of the display. Cover an inflated balloon with strips of newspaper and paste. Squeeze the newspaper in places to create 'craters'. Leave to dry before painting the moon in appropriate colours, then hang the finished moon in front of the display. Add a heading such as 'Chinese Moon Festival'.

Cover a table with yellow fabric and arrange the moon-shaped fruit in bowls on the table for the children to handle. Label each fruit.

Talk about
● Discuss the different phases of the moon and the names of the shapes.
● Talk about the shape of the different fruit on the table. Hold up one of the fruit and ask the children which phase of the moon it reminds them of.
● Talk about the significance of the shape of moon cakes.

Home links
● Invite someone who works at night to come into your setting and talk to the children about what they do.
● Send home the 'Phases of the moon' photocopiable sheet on page 73. Ask carers to encourage their children to colour in and cut out the cards before putting them in sequence to show the moon's phases.

Using the display
Knowledge and understanding of the world
● Make comparisons between day and night. Talk about the animals that prefer to come out at night. What do the children do at night? Do they know anyone who works at night?
● Introduce other examples of natural cycles. For instance, investigate the life cycle of a butterfly or frog, and discuss the changing seasons.

Physical development
● Cut up some of the fruit into small pieces for snack time.
● Make some 'moon biscuits' using round and crescent pastry cutters.

● Dramatize a trip to the moon. Curl up small and stretch up slowly as the rocket takes off. Float around in space and try to walk on the moon with big bouncy steps!

Creative development
● Create colourful moon pictures using marbling techniques on discs of paper.
● Print moons with circular objects using white paint on black paper.
● Help the children to make Chinese lanterns from folded paper.
● Enjoy a role-play visit to the moon using large boxes to create a rocket and a white sheet with cushions underneath to represent the surface of the moon.

Rosh Hashanah

Rosh Hashanah is the Jewish New Year. It is the beginning of the ten-day period leading up to the 'Day of Atonement', Yom Kippur, which is the most important time in the Jewish year. Rosh Hashanah is celebrated on two days in September or early October. Jewish people blow a 'shofar', or ram's horn, to welcome the New Year and as a remembrance of Abraham sacrificing a ram instead of his son. They exchange the greeting 'Shanah Tova' which means 'Good year' and they remember their God who created the world and who judges the things that they do in their everyday lives. Jewish people make New Year resolutions and try to find ways to change some aspect(s) of their lives for the better. At sunrise on New Year's Eve, Jewish families eat a special meal together. Honey cake or apples dipped in honey are eaten for a fruitful or sweeter New Year.

Learning objectives: to understand how sound travels; to compare loud and soft sounds.

What you need
Yellow and green backing paper; paper plates; white paper; coloured paper; paints; magazines; early years or mail order catalogues; sticky tape; glue; string; collage items including buttons, pasta and wool; paper cups; bright fabric.

What to do
Divide your display board into two sections by covering one side with yellow paper and the other with green. Make two signs, one saying 'What makes us happy?' and one saying 'What makes us sad?', and attach one to either side of the display. Talk with the children about things that make them happy or sad, then encourage them to carefully paint or draw a picture of one thing that makes them happy or sad. When all the pictures are dry, mount them on the board in the appropriate sections.

Invite the children to look through the magazines to find pictures of things that make them happy or sad. Provide help where necessary, prompting discussion. Glue the pictures onto coloured paper, then ask the children to suggest on which side of the display they should be mounted.

Give each child two paper plates and show them the collage materials. Tell them that you would like them to each make one happy and one sad face using these. Challenge them to be as imaginative as possible with their choice of materials. Use the finished paper-plate faces to make a colourful border.

Make your own versions of a shofar. Provide sheets of card and invite the children to decorate them using bright paints or crayons. When the sheets are dry, help the children to roll each one into a cone shape and secure the end using sticky tape. Arrange these on a table covered with bright fabric. Make home-made 'telephones', each from two paper cups and a length of string, and display them on the table.

Talk about
● Talk about the festival of Rosh Hashanah. Remind the children that, as this is the start of Jewish New Year, people talk about how they can change their lives for the better. Discuss ways that the children could change so that they are more helpful, look after the environment and so on.
● Jewish people often wear new outfits at Rosh Hashanah. Ask the children, 'When do you wear special clothes?'.

Home links
● Give each child a copy of the 'Happy and sad faces' photocopiable sheet on page 78 to take home. Ask carers to help their children to make a puppet with a happy face on one side and a sad face on the other.
● Invite parents to help the children to make a honey cake (see 'Mathematical development' right).

Using the display
Personal, social and emotional development
● Test the listening devices on the display table. Talk about people who are hard of hearing and, if possible, look at a selection of hearing aids. Explain that some people who are hard of hearing use sign language. Learn some simple signs.
● At Rosh Hashanah, Jewish people say sorry for the wrong things that they have done. Talk about the importance of saying sorry when you have done something wrong.

Mathematical development
● Cut some apples into halves and then into quarters and use appropriate language as you talk about a 'whole' apple, 'two halves' and 'four quarters'.
● Make a honey cake by following a basic sponge recipe and adding honey. Encourage the children to help you measure out the ingredients.

Knowledge and understanding of the world
● Help the children to cut up some apples into slices and cut out the pips. Taste an apple slice first and then dip it in honey. How does the taste change?

Creative development
● Encourage the children to use the home-made 'megaphones' on the table display to explore sound. How do voices change when speaking with and then without a megaphone?

Sukkot

Sukkot occurs in September or October and is the Jewish feast of the Tabernacles. The festival itself remembers the forty years in which Jewish people travelled in the wilderness, living in temporary huts called 'sukkahs'. During the festival today, Jewish people build a temporary shelter either at home in the garden or at the synagogue to remember this time. The shelters are built from pine branches into which flowers, fruit and vegetables are woven. The children hang fruit and vegetables inside the hut for decoration. As many meals as possible are eaten in the 'sukkah' during the festival and will include harvest fruit and vegetables.

Learning objective: to express and communicate imaginative ideas through role-play.

What you need
Yellow paper; sticks; twigs; paper; coloured tissue paper; plastic fruit and vegetables; pictures of fruit and vegetables; glue; fabric scraps;

paintbrushes; brown paint; brightly-coloured paint; large sheet; table; masking tape; small tent or table.

What to do

Tell the children that you are going to make a 'sukkah'. Cover the display board with yellow paper and paint the outline of the hut with brown paint. Use strong glue, tape or a stapler to attach twigs and sticks to the hut. Ask the children to look through magazines and to cut out pictures of fruit, vegetables or flowers. Stick these on and among the sticks and twigs. Help the children to make flowers with coloured tissue paper stuck onto discs of card. Stick these among the twigs and sticks. If you have any plastic fruit or vegetables, attach these to the 'sukkah'. Ask the children to paint some people large enough to fit inside your 'sukkah'. Label the different parts of your display and add a heading.

Arrange a large white sheet on the floor. Provide paintbrushes and brown paint, and invite the children to paint sticks and twigs onto the sheet. Allow the sheet to dry, then ask the children to add painted pictures of fruit, vegetables and flowers using thick, brightly-coloured paint. Drape the sheet over a small tent or a table to make a 'sukkah', making sure there is an open entrance at one end. The children can use the 'sukkah' for role-play.

Talk about

● Discuss the journey that the Jewish people made. Talk about journeys that the children have made. Where did they sleep during their journeys?
● Talk about temporary shelters. Have the children ever stayed in a tent or caravan? Did they enjoy it?

Home links

● Ask a carer to come into your setting to read or tell a story from their own religion to the children.
● Ask to borrow photographs of camping or caravanning holidays. Use these to make a display.

Using the display
Communication, language and literacy

● Talk to the children about the importance of the Torah to Jewish people (see the Shavuot display on page 36). Make a scroll like a Torah by rolling a sheet of paper around a pencil. Decide on something to write that is related to the chosen behaviour of the day, such as 'Today, we will help each other to tidy up'. Scribe it on the 'Torah' for the children. Change the message daily and read it together.

Knowledge and understanding of the world

● Plan a walk around your setting or local area. Draw a simple map of the route that you will take.
● Make a sukkah from cardboard boxes, twigs and leaves for small-world people. Talk about what they will need for their journeys.
● Give each child a copy of the 'Red Riding Hood's journey' photocopiable sheet on page 79. Invite them to draw a path through the woods to show Red Riding Hood's journey to Granny's house.

Physical development

● Explain that children wave flags during the festival of Sukkot. Make some simple flags with canes and thin material, or use silk scarves. Ask the children to wave the scarves or flags around in circles or up and down. (Make sure that the children stand well apart from each other if using flags on canes.)
● As part of the Sukkot celebrations, adults throw sweets for children to catch. Make some pretend sweets using play dough and sweet-wrappers and play games with them. Try to throw them into buckets or into the air to catch.
● At the end of the festival of Sukkot, the Torah is carried around the synagogue in a procession. Carry your home-made scrolls around the room in a procession. Choose a child to be a leader and ask the other children to follow the route chosen by the leader. Extend this into a *Follow-my-leader* game with actions. Let the children take turns to be the leader.

THEMES ON DISPLAY
for early years

Autumn festivals

Interactive display

fruit and vegetables

Divali

Divali, celebrated in October or November, is the Hindu festival of light and New Year. Sikh people also celebrate Divali as the time when their sixth Guru, Hargobind, was released from prison by the Mogul Emperor. Candles are lit in temples and houses to celebrate his home-coming.

Hindus commemorate the time when Rama freed his wife Sita from the demon king Ravana, and returned to their kingdom after 14 years in exile. Hindus celebrate the good winning over the evil, and light over darkness, by illuminating their homes and streets.

Hindus pray to Lakshmi, the goddess of fortune and wealth. They make rangoli patterns outside their doors and light small clay lamps, or 'divas', to welcome her into their homes. The festival lasts for five days, and during this time of new beginnings, homes are cleaned in preparation for the New Year. Women and children often decorate their hands and feet with 'mendhi' patterns.

Learning objective: to handle tools, objects and malleable materials safely and with increasing control.

What you need
Yellow backing paper; blue and green paper; newspaper; tissue paper; shiny paper; scissors; coloured foil; large potatoes; card; black paper; felt-tipped pens; sequins; glitter; paints; white sheet; night lights; clay.

What to do
Back your display board with yellow paper. Cut a large oval 'peacock's body' from green or blue paper. Scrunch up some newspaper and use it to pad out the peacock's body, before stapling it to the centre of your display.

To make the feathers, ask the children to draw around their hands on a variety of green and blue papers including tissue paper, shiny paper and foil. Help them to cut out the outlines, then attach them to the board around the peacock's body. To make the 'eyes' in the peacock's feathers, cut large potatoes in half lengthways and hollow out a disc. Ask the children to use this to print onto black paper using green and blue paints. When this is dry, cut out the shapes and stick them on top of the hand-print feathers.

Ask the children to draw around their hands on white paper and cut around the outlines. Invite them to use felt-tipped pens to decorate the shapes with flower patterns or geometric mendhi patterns. Use these to create a border for your display.

Make Divali cards with the children. Provide folded sheets of A4 card and ask the children to decorate their cards with patterned hand outlines. Alternatively, create pictures of divas and flames using scraps of coloured paper. Younger children can simply stick sequins and glitter onto hand shapes. Write greetings such as 'Subh Divali' or 'Happy Divali', then attach the cards to the display board around the peacock.

Cut mendhi patterns from paper discs and tape these to a white sheet. Help the children to paint over the paper patterns using colourful paints. When the paper is dry, remove it from the sheet, then use it to cover your display table.

Make clay divas to display on the table. Give the children a ball of clay each and ask them to press their thumbs into the ball to make a hole big enough for the candles. Once the clay divas are dry, the children can paint them and place a night light in the middle. Label the different parts of your display and add a heading.

Talk about
● Discuss the importance of light in the festival. Explain that 'Divali' means 'cluster of lights'.
● Talk about the welcome given to Rama and Sita when they returned home. Who do the children welcome into their homes?

Home links
● Make diva lamps to take home. Supply an information sheet explaining the background to the festival.
● Invite a parent or carer to prepare some Indian food for the children to taste.

Using the display
Communication, language and literacy
● Read the Hindu story of Rama and Sita to the children (see *Autumn and Winter Festivals* by Carole Court, *Themes for Early Years* series, Scholastic). Dramatize the story.
● Look at the words 'Happy Divali' written in an Indian language. Look at birthday cards and talk about what is written on them.

Mathematical development
● Look at how geometrical rangoli patterns fit together. Try fitting together plastic and wooden construction equipment to create patterns.
● Make symmetrical rangoli patterns by painting a design onto one half of a piece of paper and folding it over.

Physical development
● Outside on a hard surface, invite the children to draw large rangoli patterns using coloured chalk.
● Can the children draw patterns in wet sand, using fingers or sticks?

Creative development
● Listen to some Indian music and make up a Divali dance. Articles of Faith, tel: 0161-7636232, supply a cassette of Hindu religious music.
● Make Divali cards by cutting a diva shape from textured wallpaper and adding a flame cut from golden foil.

THEMES ON DISPLAY
for early years

Guru Nanak's Birthday

Guru Nanak was the founder of the Sikh faith. Sikhs believe that there is one God who is the maker of all things. Although Guru Nanak's birthday was in April, the celebrations are held in November when the Golden Temple of Amristar is lit with hundreds of tiny candles and lamps. The celebrations begin two days before the full moon in November and the Guru Granth Sahib (Sikh holy book) is read continuously in the 'gurdwara' (temple) followed by stories about the life and teachings of Guru Nanak. After the service, chapatis and other vegetarian food are served to everyone in the 'langar' (kitchen).

Learning objective: to recognize the value of friendship and important people in the children's lives.

What you need
Bright paper; paints; white A4 paper; coloured A4 paper; kitchen-roll tubes; yellow paint; red tissue paper; red gummed paper; card; glue; black sugar paper; pictures brought from home of people who are special to the children; books about people who help us; games that involve sharing and taking turns.

What to do
Cover the display area with brightly-coloured paper. Talk about the people that are special to the children, inviting them to share their thoughts on why these people are so important in their lives. Ask the children to paint, draw or use collage materials to create pictures of the special people in their lives. When each child has finished their picture, ask them to tell you about the people in it, and use this information to write or word-process a caption.

Mount each picture carefully, giving each a different coloured background and arranging them in an interesting, random way on the board. Attach the children's captions next to their pictures. Make candles to use as a border of light around the children's pictures. Ask them to paint cardboard kitchen-roll tubes with yellow paint. When these are dry, add flames made from scrunched-up pieces of red tissue paper or gummed paper scraps stuck onto flame shapes made from card.

Place a table near to the display. Ask the children to bring in photographs of their families and other people who are special to them. Look at them in turn and take time to discuss individual photographs. Display them on the table in a home-made album with a description against each picture

explaining who the person is and why they are special. Display books about people who help us, and games which involve sharing and taking turns.

Talk about

● Discuss Guru Nanak's belief that everyone is important. Think of something that each child contributes to the group, such as kindness, a smiling face or being helpful to other children.
● Ask each of the children to choose a special person to talk about to the rest of the group.

Home links

● Invite a parent or carer to come into your setting to make chapatis with the children.
● Discuss the children's photographs during circle time.

Here is my Grandad and all my friends at Nursery. My Grandad is special. I look after him because he has a broken arm.
Jordan B

Using the display

Personal, social and emotional development.

● Talk about being kind to each other. How can the children be helpful at your setting? Make a list of their suggestions. Make another list of helpful things that the children can do at home.
● Play games involving sharing and taking turns.
● Make an imitation cake from a cardboard box. Let the children decorate it, and add candles to light on the children's birthdays.

Mathematical development

● Make a birthday graph to display. Talk about which month has the most birthdays. Are there any months with no birthdays? Do any children share their birthday month with Guru Nanak?
● Play a card game such as *Snap* and talk about the importance of sharing cards equally and taking turns. Deal out the cards one by one and then count

how many cards each child has at the start of the game. Do they have the same number? How can you ensure they are the same? Talk about 'taking away' and 'adding another'.

Knowledge and understanding of the world

● Make chapatis with the children. Notice the changes that occur as the ingredients are mixed and then cooked.
● Make model temples from cardboard boxes. Stick coloured foil discs around the walls to represent the hundreds of lamps lit on Guru Nanak's birthday.
● To celebrate Guru Nanak's birthday, Sikhs enjoy a feast at which they eat vegetarian food. Try making a dip using natural yoghurt and freshly-chopped mint. Cut some slices of cucumber and dip them into the mixture. Talk about the sour taste and compare it with the sweet flavour of ready-prepared fruit yoghurt. (**NB** Check for food allergies and dietary requirements.)

THEMES ON DISPLAY
for early years

Harvest baskets

Learning objective: to understand the importance of sharing what we have with others.

What you need
Two tables; fabric; mushroom baskets; shoeboxes; card; blue wrapping paper or crêpe paper; scissors; tissue paper; sticky tape; harvest gifts brought by the children; shallow plastic trays to store the gifts; ice-cream containers; vase of flowers; grain; wheat.

What to do
Discuss the harvest gifts and decide how they can be divided up between the baskets so that each basket contains a range of items. With the children, make labels for each of the types of produce that you have, for example, 'tins', 'boxes', 'fruit', 'vegetables' and so on. Arrange storage trays on one of the tables and place one label next to each tray. Encourage the children to sort their gifts onto the appropriate trays.

Give each child a mushroom basket and help them to cover it with blue wrapping paper or crêpe paper, securing with sticky tape. Invite the children to scrunch up some tissue paper and to place it in the bottom of their baskets, then let each child

choose one thing from each tray and arrange the chosen items in their basket. Share out any items left on the trays. Cover a second table with fabric and arrange the baskets on top. Decide who will be the recipients of the baskets, and write a caption. Display some samples of grain and wheat, and arrange a vase of fresh flowers on the table beside the food baskets.

Talk about
● Discuss the importance of sharing with others and caring for those who need our help.
● Talk about the categories for the food items on the trays.

Home links
● Invite parents and carers to accompany the children as they distribute their baskets.

Further display table ideas
● Set up a market stall table with salt-dough and papier-mâché fruit and vegetables made by the children.
● Have a table of foods which grow under the ground, preferably still with their roots and leaves, for the children to handle and smell.
● Make a scarecrow and pumpkin lantern with the children, and place them beside the display.

Winter festivals

Candles

Learning objectives: to investigate candles; to understand that it is dangerous to play with candles and matches.

What you need
Bright backing paper; contrasting border paper; reflective paper; coloured paper; coloured sugar paper; newspaper; brightly-coloured paints; glitter; collage materials; cardboard tubes; gold paper; clay or salt dough; a selection of candles, including floating and perfumed candles; red and yellow fabric.

What to do
Back the display board with colourful paper. Add a contrasting border and decorate it with shiny flame shapes cut from reflective paper. Cut a large candle shape from coloured sugar paper and fasten it to the display board, padding it out with newspaper to create a 3-D effect.

Ask the children to make a decorative flame using coloured paper, glitter and other collage materials.

Invite the children to create individual candles by decorating cardboard tubes with colourful paper scraps and collage materials. Staple these to the board. Discuss words associated with candles and flames. Write individual words onto cut-out flame shapes. Mount the shapes on gold paper and display one above each of the children's candles. Add a title to your display.

Place a fabric-covered table in front of the display, and arrange your collection of candles on it. Invite the children to describe the candles, then add appropriate labels. Ask them to make candle-holders from clay or salt dough, to sprinkle them with glitter while wet, and to paint them when dry. Arrange the children's candle-holders among the candles on the table.

Talk about
● Reinforce the dangers of lit candles, flames and hot wax. Remind the children that they must never go near a candle or any other flame without adult supervision.
● Why are some candles perfumed? Light a perfumed candle and leave it on a high shelf. Do the children like the smell, or do they prefer non-scented candles?

Home links
● Ask parents and carers to emphasize the dangers of playing with matches and candles.
● Ask for contributions of decorative or unusual candles for your display.

From flickering candles to giant pancakes, the display ideas in this chapter capture the excitement and colour of a variety of winter festivals including St Lucia's Day, Hanukkah and Christmas.

THEMES ON DISPLAY
for early years

Hanukkah

The Jewish festival of Hanukkah is usually in December and begins on the 25th day of the Jewish month Kislev. It is a family occasion where relatives gather together to give thanks to their god, sing traditional Jewish songs and exchange cards and gifts. In 167BC, the Greeks ruled over the Jewish land of Israel. The son of an old Jewish priest, Judah of Maccabee, was the leader of a Jewish army who drove the Greeks from Israel. The Greeks left the Jewish temple with only enough oil to keep their sacred lamp burning for a day. The Jewish God miraculously kept the lamp burning for the eight days it took for a messenger to return with more oil. Every year, Jews remember this miracle by lighting a new candle on each day of the festival. A 'menorah' (a seven-branched candelabrum) or a 'hanukiah' (a nine-branched lamp) is placed in the window. The ninth candle (the 'shamash') is used as a 'servant' to light the other eight candles. Food eaten during the festival is fried in oil to commemorate the miracle of the oil burning in the temple.

Learning objective: to use number names in order and count reliably using everyday objects.

What you need
Blue backing paper; brown paper; gold foil; red and yellow Cellophane; yellow tissue paper; card; glue; strips of black paper; paper straws; foil; brown, yellow and red paints; sponge; potato; patterned fabric; information books about Hanukkah, such as *All about Hanukkah* by Judyth Groner and Madeline Wikler (Kar-Ben Copies) and *Hanukkah Fun* by Judy Bastyra (Kingfisher Books).

What to do
Back the display board with blue paper and make a window sill by attaching brown paper across the bottom. Create individual windowpanes using

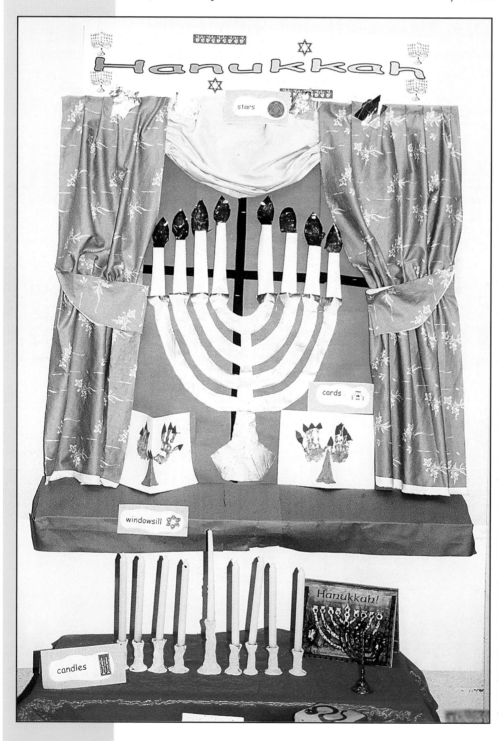

strips of black paper. Cut a hanukiah from gold foil and mount it on the 'window sill'. Make candles from white card to stick onto the candle-holders on the hanukiah, and add flames cut from red and yellow Cellophane.

Create Hanukkah cards with the children to put along the 'window sill'. Fold a piece of card in half. Ask the children to make a hanukiah by making handprints with yellow or orange paint on either side of the fold. Overlap the two thumbprints down the fold of the card to make the 'shamash'. Stick coloured tissue or foil 'flames' onto the fingertips and paint on a candlestick base.

Show the children how to make the Jewish Star of David using different techniques. For example, cut foil into triangles and stick two pieces together to make a star shape, or make star prints with potato or sponge. Help the children to cut out their star shapes and attach them to the display to form a border. Add a heading above your display, decorated with Stars of David, and label the different parts of the display. To make the window look more effective, hang patterned fabric 'curtains'

around it. In front of the display, place a table and cover it with fabric. Represent a hanukiah by making nine clay or salt-dough candle-holders with the children, and painting them yellow. Put a candle in each holder with a larger 'shamash' in the centre. Display books about Hanukkah on the table.

On a second smaller table, display examples of commercial and home-made games involving dice or spinners. Make 'dreidels' (traditional four-sided tops) or use discs of card and a pencil to make spinners.

Talk about
● Discuss how the festival of Hanukkah began and make comparisons with other festivals of light.
● Talk about the games that the children play at home.

Home links
● Send home a sheet explaining the main points of the festival.
● Draw a hanukiah and number each candle to create a counting sheet for the children to take home.

Using the display
Communication, language and literacy
● Introduce vocabulary associated with light and dark. Make lists of all the relevant words that the children can suggest. Use your list to create a group poem.
● Discuss and listen to others talking about the anticipation of a special event such as a birthday.

Mathematical development
● Invite the children to play commercially-produced and home-made games involving dice and spinners.

Knowledge and understanding of the world
● Find a recipe for potato latkes. Cook them with the children and discuss the changes that take place as the potato is cooked in the oil.
● Talk about how the children's families use oil in cooking. Make a simple salad dressing with oil and vinegar and sprinkle over shredded lettuce.

Creative development
● Use malleable materials to make candle-holders.
● Use paper straws to create Star of David mobiles.

Advent

The word 'Advent' comes from the Latin word 'coming' and is a time of anticipation and preparation for the Christian celebration of Christmas. Advent Sunday is the fourth Sunday before Christmas Day, and is the start of the Christian year. It is a time when Christians think about the coming of Jesus into the world as a baby, and prepare to celebrate his birthday.

Christian children associate Advent with calendars, which are used to count down the days until the birth of Jesus Christ on Christmas Day.

Learning objective: to count and recognize numbers to 10 and beyond.

What you need

Red paper; 24 small cereal boxes; Christmas wrapping paper; split-pin paper fasteners; scissors; glue; white sticky labels; white paint; salt dough; thin ribbon; cardboard boxes; small artificial Christmas tree; Christmas decorations.

What to do

Start by looking at an Advent calendar and talking about the Advent period. Tell the children that you are going to make your own giant calendar.

Cover the display board with red paper and paint blobs of 'snow' using white paint. Make Christmas parcels with the children by gluing Christmas wrapping paper around small cereal boxes. Cut a large door in the front of

each parcel and make handles using split-pin paper fasteners. Number the parcels from 1 to 24 using sticky labels.

Sort the boxes into number order and into six rows of four. Attach them in this order to the display board using drawing pins. Ask the children to help you to make 24 pendants from salt dough. Roll out the dough and cut it into Christmas shapes such as bells, holly and stars, using modelling tools. Pierce a hole in each shape with a pencil and write a number on each, up to 24, using a pencil. Children can also write the initial letter of their name if they wish. Bake the shapes in a low oven until hard. When the shapes are cold and dry, let the children paint them and then attach lengths of thin ribbon. Put a 'pendant' into each of the parcels on the display.

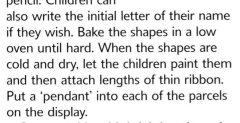

Cover a table with brightly-coloured fabric and put a small Christmas tree in the centre. Let the children help to decorate it. Each day, invite a child to open the appropriately-numbered door, take out the pendant and hang it on the tree. Help them to make 'Christmas presents' by wrapping different-shaped cardboard boxes with Christmas paper and placing them under the tree.

Talk about
● Talk about the anticipation of Christmas. What do the children most look forward to?
● Ask the children if there are other occasions they look forward to, such as birthdays and holidays.
● Talk about family preparations for Christmas, such as buying presents, baking and cleaning the house.

Home links
● Ask parents and carers to donate tree decorations, wrapping paper and small cereal boxes.
● Invite parents and carers to come in to help to make the salt-dough pendants with the children.

Using the display
Personal, social and emotional development
● Make a simple board game based on the 24 days until Christmas. Use a dice numbered 1, 2, 3, 1, 2, 3. These indicate the number of spaces that can be moved on each throw. Stick pictures cut from old Christmas cards along the 24 squares, and use Christmas cake decorations as counters.
● Make a large 'Advent board' using a sheet of white paper divided into 24 squares. Number the squares, leaving space for writing. Each day, choose a child to think of some way in which they have been helpful, such as tidying up or sharing toys. Write this in the square.

Mathematical development
● Make some number cards from 1 to 24 and attach string to the top of each card. Choose a child to find the card that matches the number on the parcel 'door' and pendant each day. Tie the card alongside the pendants on the line. Remember to add extra pendants and cards after the weekends to ensure the numbers are in order and match the date.
● Introduce the appropriate words to depict order as you open the parcels, for example, 'first', 'fourth' and so on.

Creative development
● Make a star mobile, adding a star to a string suspended across the room each day. Use different materials to create the stars, such as fabric, hologram paper, Cellophane, art straws, glitter and foil.
● Give each child a paper plate and ask them to draw what they think their faces will be like on Christmas morning. Write each child's name on their plate, and then number the plates from 1 to 24. Pin them along a display board facing the wall. Each day, turn over one plate and talk about who drew the face and what it might be thinking about.

Christmas

Christians celebrate Christmas on 25 December as they remember the birth of Jesus Christ. Children perform Nativity plays telling the story of how Jesus was born in a stable and how the shepherds and Three Wise Men followed a bright star to find the baby, bringing him gifts.

Children usually believe that Father Christmas brings presents for them on Christmas morning. Christmas is a time when Christian families and friends join together and celebrate the birth of Jesus Christ.

Learning objective: to develop a respect for one's own culture and for other people's cultures.

What you need
Display surface against a wall or window; silver and gold foil; painting paper; paints in various colours; collage materials; paper in various colours; fabric scraps; corrugated card; cardboard boxes in different shapes and sizes; straw; books

about Christmas such as *The Story of Christmas* by Jane Ray (Orchard Books) and *The Good Little Christmas Tree* by Ursula Moray Williams (Walker Books).

What to do
Cover the base and back wall of your display area with dark backing paper. Share the books with the children and talk about the story of the Nativity. Tell the children that you are going to make a Nativity scene using their paintings of the different characters and animals. Ask the children to work in pairs or small groups, and decide which group is going to paint which character. Provide plenty of A3 paper and then let the children paint their characters, encouraging them to use the whole of the paper so that all the characters are roughly the same size. The group painting Jesus should also paint his crib.

When the paintings are dry, invite the children to add details such as crowns, decorated clothes and so on, using collage materials. Give the animals textured coats by adding cotton wool, wool and other fabric scraps. Attach

around the stable floor. Stick some inside the crib to make a bed for Jesus. Suspend the angels above the display using strong thread. Provide a large pre-cut star shape and ask the children to cover it with silver foil. Suspend this, together with smaller star shapes created in the same way, above the display. Label each character and add an appropriate title.

Talk about
● Talk about the Christmas story and the traditions associated with Christmas.
● Talk about Christmas in other countries. Discuss the clothes that people wear in hot countries and compare them to the clothes that the Nativity figures are dressed in and the clothes that the children are wearing.

Home links
● Organize a carol service and invite parents and carers to come and join in with the singing.

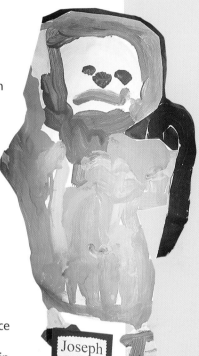

Joseph

each figure to an appropriately-sized cardboard box so that they can be moved around the display area.

Create a stable by painting a cardboard box and a sheet of corrugated card in shades of brown. When dry, use the box as the wall of the stable and attach the corrugated card to form the roof. Invite the children to arrange the straw

Using the display
Personal, social and emotional development
● Talk about the need to treat new babies with care and concern.
● Why do babies cry? Talk about the children's emotions. Explore with them what makes them cry.
● Visit a home for the elderly to sing Christmas carols and songs.

Communication, language and literacy
● Introduce new vocabulary associated with the story.
● Learn some Christmas rhymes together and share Christmas books.

Mathematical development
● Discuss the position of the stars above the display. Which is the highest?
● Look at the shape of the stars above the display. Invite the children to count the points of each star. Make patterns by printing star shapes.

Knowledge and understanding of the world
● Mary and Joseph travelled to Bethlehem on a donkey. The Three Wise Men travelled on camels. Make comparisons between past and present modes of travels. How would they travel today?

Physical development
● Dramatize the Nativity story with the children. Move like donkeys and camels. Stretch up to point to the star and climb up and down hillsides. Rock Jesus to sleep.

Creative development
● Learn some new Christmas songs and accompany the singing with musical instruments.

THEMES ON DISPLAY *for early years*

Chinese New Year

The Chinese New Year festival lasts for fifteen days during January and February. The date is determined by a new moon. Each year is dedicated to a different animal on a twelve-year cycle. In the traditional story, each of the twelve animals wanted to have the year named after themselves, so they decided to settle the argument with a race across the river. The rat won, even though it was through cheating, and so the first year of the cycle of twelve years was named after him.

Before the New Year festival, people clean their homes to wash away bad luck. Red good-luck decorations are hung around the home and children are given 'lucky money' envelopes. During the festival, there are street processions, fireworks and lion dancing, and the streets are decorated with flags, banners and lanterns.

Learning objective: to explore colour, texture, shape and form in two and three dimensions.

What you need
Black and gold paper; white A4

paper; card; red and white fabric or traditional Chinese clothes; bright crayons or pens; paints; two clean mousse pots; red and orange tissue paper; cardboard boxes; books such as *Cleversticks* by Bernard Ashley (Picture Lions), *Dat's New Year* by Linda Smith (A & C Black) and *C is for China* by Sungwan So (Frances Lincoln); Chinese cooking utensils.

What to do
This display is ideal for an unusual position such as a window recess, where different light patterns will shine across the brightly-coloured materials. Place a table or other display surface in front of the area.

Make costumes by cutting red and white fabric into the shape of trousers and shirts and sticking the fabric onto card. Hang the home-made or real Chinese costumes at either side of the display. Ask the children to make some Chinese lanterns. Encourage them to draw patterns onto strips of paper using bright crayons or pens. Help them to cut out random shapes from their paper and then tape the two short ends together to create a cylinder. Add a paper handle at the top and tissue paper strips around the bottom. Suspend the lanterns, together with real examples if you have them, above the display.

Invite small groups of children to paint colourful Chinese dragons. When the pictures are dry, mount them on bright paper before adding them to your display. Have a go at reproducing some Chinese writing and add this to the display.

Make a three-dimensional Chinese dragon by painting cardboard boxes in various shades of green before fixing them together. Add flames to the dragon's mouth using red and orange tissue paper. Ask the children to paint mousse pots with black paint to make the eyes (it is thought to be bad luck to put the eyes onto the dragon until the actual day). Use green triangular card to make the ears. Place the dragon's head on the display surface. Arrange a series of boxes behind the dragon's head to represent its body, and cover these boxes with red fabric.

Display the books and cooking utensils in front of the dragon. Cut gold discs to make 'lucky money' or use foil-wrapped chocolate coins and place them in an open red envelope at the front of the display. Label the different elements of your display and add an appropriate title.

Talk about
● Talk about dragons, explaining that they are not real creatures. Name together some other mythical characters, such as unicorns, griffins and giants.
● Discuss the clothes on the display. Make comparisons with the children's own clothes.
● Find out more about the tradition of 'lucky money' in red envelopes.

Home links
● Ask parents to introduce the children to Chinese food by visiting a Chinese restaurant, buying a take-away meal or cooking noodles and rice at home.

Using the display
Personal, social and emotional development
● Talk about the different animals represented each year. Work out the animals for the years in which the children were born, and make a display depicting this. Add your own birth year to the display!
● Read *Cleversticks* and talk about how the boy in the story could use chopsticks well. Discuss things that the children can do well.

Communication, language and literacy
● Look at a menu from a Chinese restaurant and try to copy some of the writing.
● Create a Chinese restaurant role-play area.

Knowledge and understanding of the world
● Make comparisons between raw and cooked rice. Investigate texture, appearance, smell and taste.
● Put raw noodles in the water tray and discuss what happens to them.

Physical development
● Cover some children in a sheet to represent a dragon. Can they walk around in a group? Try some winding, stretching and bending movements.

St Lucia's Day

St Lucia's Day on 13 December marks the start of the Christmas celebrations for Christians in some European countries. St Lucia, a Christian originally from Sicily, was killed by the Romans because of her religious beliefs. 'Lucia' means 'light', and in Italy St Lucia's Day is celebrated with a fire festival which includes a procession by candle-light.

In Sweden, every town has a Lucia Queen who wears a long white dress with a red sash. On her head, she wears a halo of evergreen twigs and seven lit candles. St Lucia is the patron saint of light, represented by the candles, and the evergreen twigs symbolize continuing life throughout the winter.

Boys and girls dressed in white accompany the Lucia Queen as she visits houses and hospitals in the town. The girls wear tinsel in their hair and the boys wear cone-shaped hats decorated with shiny stars. People eat special festival biscuits called Lussekatter, which are shaped like the letter 's'.

Learning objective: to begin to recognize letters by their shape and sound.

What you need
Black and white paper; large white sheet; red ribbon; evergreen branches; large gold and silver stars; reflective paper; salt dough; white and yellow card; string; wool; glue; painting paper; painting materials.

Using the display
Personal, social and emotional development
● Discuss occasions when the children wear special clothes. How do they feel when they wear these clothes?
● Invite the children to bring in a favourite outfit and hold your own St Lucia's Parade (have some spare clothes ready). Choose a child to lead the procession. Play music as you process around the room and finish with a feast of the Lussekatter (see the recipe on page 80).

Communication, language and literacy
● Identify things in your display that start with 's', such as 'sash', 'stars' and 'seven' (candles). Give each child a 'Starting with "s"' photocopiable sheet (page 75). Ask them to identify and colour in the items that start with 's'.

Mathematical development
● Focus on number 7 by making an interest table. Arrange seven candles in the centre and ask children to add things relating to the number 7, for example, birthday cards, plastic and foam numerals, dominoes with dots that add up to 7, or sets of seven objects.
● Learn the names of the days of the week in the correct sequence.
● Make cards numbered 1 to 7 to play with and arrange next to groups of small objects.

Knowledge and understanding of the world
● Use the photocopiable sheet on page 80 to make some Lussekatter, or use the basic bread recipe to make 's'-shaped dough buns. Discuss the changes that occur as the ingredients are mixed together, kneaded and heated.

What to do
Cover the display board with black paper. Ask a child to lie down on a large sheet of white paper and draw around him or her. Cut out the outline and invite the children to choose a skin tone to paint the outline. Add facial features using collage materials and use strands of wool to make hair.

Make a dress shape from white sheeting and staple this to the outline. Add a red ribbon or shiny paper sash. Attach the outline to the board. Staple some pieces of evergreen branches to the figure's head and add seven candles cut from white card.

Make 's' shapes using thick wool, salt dough, string, paint and reflective paper and glue them to squares of red and yellow card. Use the cards to form a border, then fill in any spaces with gold and silver stars.

Ask the children to paint pictures of the Lucia Queen and her attendants. Mount them on yellow paper and attach them around the display. Make a large title which says 'St Lucia's Day' and place it at the top.

Set up a table near to the display and cover it with paper. Arrange on it the resources needed to make cones and crown shapes. Supply white card, aprons, glue, scissors, gold and silver stars and sequins and invite the children to decorate their own head-dresses.

Talk about
● Discuss with the children the clothes that kings and queens wear.
● Look around your setting to find things that begin with the letter 's'.

Home links
● Encourage carers to help their children find items that begin with 's' at home. Ask them to let their children bring these in to add to a display table.

Pancake Day

Pancake Day is the popular name for Shrove Tuesday, the day before Ash Wednesday, which marks the beginning of the Christian period of Lent. This is the time of reflection before Easter when Christians traditionally abstain from eating meat, fat, eggs and dairy products. On Shrove Tuesdays in the past, people used up the contents of store cupboards instead of wasting them. Pancakes were an easy and tasty way to do this.

Learning objective: to talk about likes and dislikes.

What you need
Wallpaper; textured paper; brown and yellow paint; white card; collage materials; white paper; crayons; chalk; paper plates; fabric; scraps of vinyl flooring; kitchen scales; bucket balance; three seed trays; *The Big Pancake* (*Favourite Tales* series, Ladybird Books).

What to do
Read *The Big Pancake* to the children and talk about Pancake Day. Have any of the children eaten pancakes before? Did they like them? Suggest that you make a display which includes elements from the story.

Cover the display board with wallpaper, or print your own, to represent a kitchen. Cut out some discs in two different sizes, approximately 10cm and 15cm in diameter, and invite the children to paint them to represent pancakes. Arrange them alternately around the edge of the display to form a border. Reserve some of the discs for the table activities. Cut out a rectangle from textured paper and paint it brown to represent a table-top. Attach it to one side of the display.

Ask seven children to decorate one paper plate each to represent the faces of the hungry boys. Attach the completed faces around the 'table'. Make the boys' mother by drawing around a child on a large sheet of white paper. Invite the children to add the facial features, clothes and hair using their choice of collage materials. Attach the figure to the display board next to the table. Number seven pieces of card from 1 to 7 and attach one next to each paper-plate 'face' around the 'table'.

Make a large circular pancake from card, and ask the children to decorate it with brown and yellow painted blobs and streaks to look like a pancake. Stick it in the centre of the 'table'.

In front of the display, place a fabric-covered table. Cut out several discs in three different sizes (small, medium and large) from the scraps of vinyl flooring. Arrange them in size order in shallow containers, such as seed trays. Include the card discs left from the wall displays.

Arrange some resources for weighing the 'pancakes' such as kitchen scales and a bucket balance. Label the items on the table and add a main heading for the display.

Talk about
● Discuss the story of The Big Pancake. When do the children feel hungry?
● Talk about how pancakes are made. Together, try to recall the sequence of events as the boys made the pancakes in the story.

Home links
● Invite parents and carers in to help the children make some pancakes.

Using the display
Communication, language and literacy
● Find a pancake recipe and discuss the ingredients together.
● Make a shopping list of ingredients that are needed to make pancakes. Include some favourite fillings!
● Say the poem 'The Pancake' by Christina Rossetti from This Little Puffin... compiled by Elizabeth Matterson (Puffin Books) and make up appropriate actions.

Mathematical development
● Make seven small pancakes from card and match them to seven small-world figures.
● Work with seven children to follow a home-made recipe card and the sequence in the story to make some pancakes. Help two children to crack the eggs (ensure that they wash their hands after handling the eggs), two to measure the milk, two to weigh the flour and one to stir the mixture. Talk about the number of children, the quantity of milk, flour and eggs, and the number of pancakes made.
● Let the children explore the 'pancakes' on the table and try to weigh them. Can they make the

buckets on the scales balance? Introduced the words 'heavy', 'light' and 'balance'.

Knowledge and understanding of the world
● Make some pancakes and experiment with different toppings. Make a graph of favourite toppings using card outlines of appropriately-coloured pancakes.
● Talk about changes in the ingredients as they are mixed and heated.

Physical development
● Pretend to toss pancakes in a pan. Use toy frying pans and try to toss the imitation pancakes on the table display.
● Dramatize the story of The Big Pancake, taking the parts of the children, the mother and the animals. Discuss with the children how each animal would move.

Bird's Christmas tree

Learning objective: to handle tools and materials safely and with increasing control.

What you need
Branch; small plant pot; plaster of Paris; white paint; glitter; washing-tablet bags; lard; seed; cake; breadcrumbs; biscuit pieces; yoghurt pots; pan; bowl; spoons; heat source.

What to do
Paint the branch white and sprinkle on glitter while the paint is still wet. Mix the plaster of Paris according to the instructions, and pour some in the bottom of a plant pot, making sure the hole is sealed first. Stick the branch into the plaster and allow it to set. Away from the children, melt the lard and allow it to cool, but not set. Pour it into a large bowl and invite the children to add small seeds, crumbled cake, biscuit pieces and breadcrumbs. Take turns to put some into a yoghurt pot.

When set, tip out the bird cakes. Give each child a washing-tablet bag to put their bird cake into. Hang the bird cakes on your 'Christmas tree'. Instead of washing-tablet bags, you could put the bird cake mixture into discs of net, tied at the top with string.

Stand the tree on a table covered with white fabric or cotton wool to represent snow. Surround the tree with pictures of birds and bird feeders. Make a sign for the table from folded card saying 'Remember the birds at Christmas Time'. Just before

Christmas, let the children take their bird cakes home to hang outside on Christmas Day.

Talk about:
● Discuss the special foods that the children will eat at Christmas.
● Talk about the problems that birds have finding food at Christmas time.

Home links
● Send home the recipe for bird cake.
● Ask parents to hang up the 'cake' and encourage the children to talk about the kinds of birds that eat the food.

Further table display ideas
● Invite the children to create a 'family gift' tree display by hanging Cellophane parcels of small home-made sweets on a painted branch.
● Create a decorated tree display. Let the children mould and paint salt-dough decorations and then hang them from a painted branch.

Phases of the moon

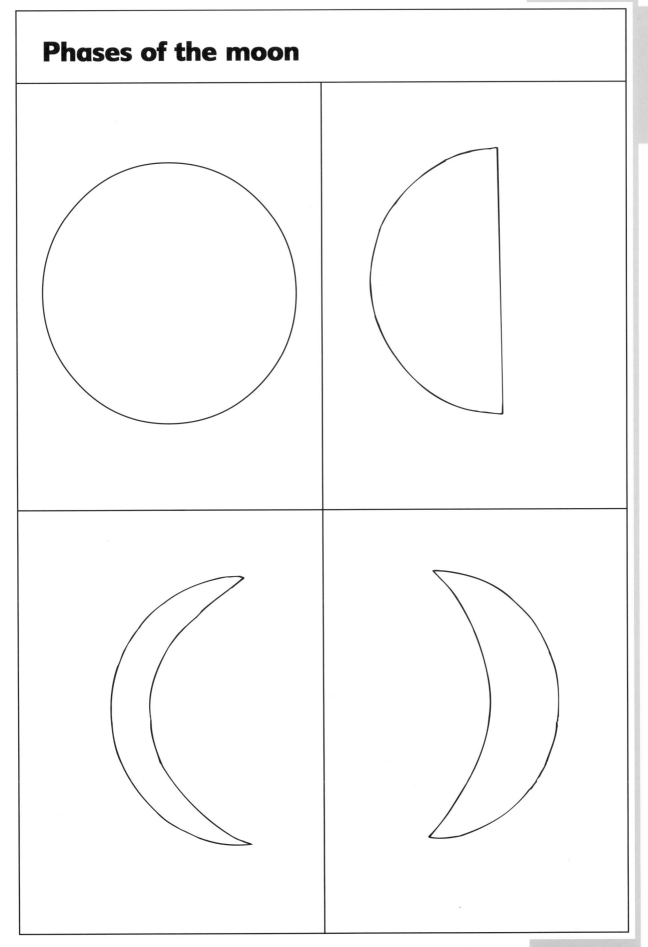

Growth of a seed

Starting with 's'

Kindness certificate

Today _____

_____

_____

Signed _____

Date _____

Make your own rakhis

Happy and sad faces

Make a stick puppet using a cheese box. Stick the two sides of the box together. Cover each surface with pale paper and ask your child to draw a happy face on one side and a sad face on the other. Alternatively, cut out features from coloured paper and stick them to each side of the box. Glue on some woollen hair and attach a lollipop-stick 'neck'. Hold the puppet by the stick and turn it round to represent happy and sad moods.

Red Riding Hood's journey

Recipe for Lussekatter

Equipment
● For each child: small bowl; wooden spoon; apron; board.
● To share: greased baking sheet; wire cooling rack; two bowls; fork.

Ingredients
● 325g flour
● quarter of a teaspoon of baking powder
● 2 eggs
● 125g sugar
● 250g margarine
● vanilla essence

What to do
● Wash hands and put on aprons.
● Pre-heat the oven to Gas Mark 4 (350 °F).
● Put the sugar and margarine in a bowl and mix together.
● In a separate bowl, beat the eggs and gradually add to the mixture.
● Gradually add a few drops of vanilla essence.
● Use hands to work in the flour and baking powder slowly until well mixed.
● Divide the dough into balls.
● Roll each ball into a long sausage shape.
● Curl the sausage shapes into 's' shapes.
● Arrange biscuits on a baking sheet and bake in the oven for up to 10 minutes.
● Wash hands.
● Remove biscuits from oven and cool on a wire rack.